The

The Power of...
What Is
Love??

Motivator
Mikkita L Moore

The Power of... What Is Love??

ISBN: 978-1-7354792-7-9
Imprint: Invisible Daughter, LLC
Printed and bounded in the United States of America.

The Power of... What Is Love??

<u>Thank You!!</u>

The Power of... What Is Love??

Special Thanks &
Dedication

Thank all of you for making this book possible

All the Authors: *Mikkita L Moore, Latonya Willett, Morgana Matthews, Francesca Cole-Barnes, Timothia Reid, Nikita Nicole, Risa Jenkins, Tonia Reaves, Luberta Lytle, Antoinette B. Seawood, Q.R. Williams!!*

Graphic Designer: *Shawn Robinson, of 727 Marketing... It's been a pleasure to work with you!!*

Editor: *Tiffany Jasper... Thank You for always making sure Invisible Daughter, LLC books are "write" ....*

Thank you for being an amazing friend, and sister on top of being an amazing PERSON!

This book is dedicated to all the People that has ever battled with being loved, feeling love, wanting love.... Know that YOU ARE A CONQUEROR....

YOU ARE LOVE!

This one is for you!

The Power of... What Is Love??

The Power of... What Is Love??

Table of Contents

Chapter One: Love is Just Different for Me, **Mikkita L. Moore**

Chapter Two: The Core of Loving Thyself, **Antoinette B. Seawood**

Chapter Three: You Can't Teach What You Don't Know, **Nikita Nicole**

Chapter Four: To Be Loved… Oh What A Feeling, To Be Loved, **Francesca Cole-Barnes**

Chapter Five: Unconditional Love, **Timothia Reid**

Chapter Six: Love Is the Greatest Gift, **Morgana Matthews**

Chapter Seven: Iridescent Kisses, **Q. R. Williams**

Chapter Eight: Learning to Love Myself Better, **Tonia Reaves**

Chapter Nine: Exhale, **Risa Jenkins**

Chapter Ten: The Different Levels of Love, **Latonya Willett**

Chapter Eleven: Loving Me Some Me, **Luberta Lytle**

The Power of... What Is Love??

The Power of... What Is Love??

ENJOY....

The Power of... What Is Love??

Chapter One:

Love is Just Different for Me

Mikkita L. Moore

Mikkita L Moore, an author, international motivational speaker and mother of five, starting at the tender age of 14 from the South Side of Chicago. Mikkita is the Founder and CEO of *The Art of Transparency, NFP* an organization with a vision and mission to "Heal ONE Person, One City, ONE State, ONE Nation at a time. We provide the pivotal tools resources and fundamental needs necessary to create lasting impact for those affected by various traumas.". The CEO of *Invisible Daughter, LLC* a publishing and Writing Coach Company. Although passionate about teaching others about her journey which includes forgiving a father that wasn't, in her opinion, able to be the model man she had desperately needed as a young girl growing into womanhood, she continued to struggle with her inner feelings. Being able to convey these imbedded emotions is also comforting for her. Learning the *Art of Transparency* is equivalent to facing and being fully aware of who she is, her ability to candidly speak from the heart about real life issues and how to conquer life's trials is one of my greatest gifts.

Speaking to participants is a time for meaningful engagement. Time used to encourage, lead and offer real life situations and results to enable listeners to truly understand and connect with her, not only as the speaker but to have empathy for the topic. One of the results that Mikkita obtains when speaking to audiences is her dynamic ability to ignite an awakening within those who hear her story. It allows them to realize and understand their issue more clearly, that she has been through similar situations and how they, too, can overcome the feelings and possible stagnations from its impact. These processes are all facilitated with audience in mind.

How beneficial it is to have the skill to ignite the path of change. Mikkita's niche is engaging her audience with realistic topics that help identify the issues and the willingness to work towards resolutions. Her first two books, *The Letter From, the Invisible Daughter* as well as *The Cause and Effect of The Invisible Daughter,* talks about, among other topics, parenting a child that's different from the rest and her doubts of being a good mother. As she speaks candidly about her thoughts of suicide and being in unsafe relationships that included domestic violence; emotional, mental and physical, she creates and implements strategies to be used in the moment to begin healing processes for others. Most gatherings include hands-on activities. There's only room for results; a growth mindset. Mikkita continues to receive multiple invites to speak due this direct approach which call for peace and progress in the lives of others.

During the pandemic of 2020, Mikkita was blessed to birth another seven books through collaborations with other Authors, giving her a total of nine published books. In the words of Mikkita about what inspired he to write her books... *With all of my books I wanted to reach my audience on a level that's different from the rest. I needed to reach an audience that hasn't heard about the Black girl from the south side of Chicago that wasn't poor and not knowing where her next meal would come from. The girl that her mother wasn't a drug addict, father wasn't a drug pusher. I was tired of the stereo types that I had to be from this type of family or that kind of family because I had my first child at the age of 14 years old. My all-time favorite was the one that says teenage moms can't raise their children effectively or the one that says teenage moms are all high school drop outs. Neither of which proves true for me.*

My books are not about the average poor Black girl living in poverty. My book is about my life, from a perspective of a teenage mom that didn't struggle, that didn't drop out of high school but in fact graduated high school a year ahead of time with honors. This book is my life from a perspective that thought about suicide, went through domestic violence, emotionally mentally and physically. This book talks from a perspective of not feeling the love of my father searching for that type of love from boys/men that either couldn't give it or just didn't know how to give love.

My books talk about parenting a child that's different from the rest of her five children. Wondering where I went wrong as a parent, or as a real mother. I talk about being fatherless and how that affects my relationships with men.

In my books I talk about how my struggle with alcohol was the only way I could cope with the depression and anger that was built from all the "life issues" that I didn't know how to let go of. My books come from real life situations that happens in our community far too often and over looked because it's not society's "norm".

Mikkita along with The Art of Transparency, NFP tour has scheduled and appeared for several presentations and speaking engagements, over the last five years with heightened interest in each state. Moving forward there will be plans to host expos, workshops and conferences on trauma healing and awareness. This tour has touched over 950,000 lives through the AOT tour platform, the AOT talk/radio show, as well as their community outreach.

Love is Just Different for Me...

Talking about love has always been a sore subject with me. At an early age I realized that Love equates to abandonment. Every one that said that they loved me, abandoned me in one way or another.

When I was younger, I lived with my aunt and uncle which I originally thought were my mom and dad... (Read the first book, The Letter, From the Invisible Daughter" to get that story). My aunt was a housewife and my uncle was the provider, she was a house wife in every sense of the word. She made sure the kids were fed, bathed and their homework was done. Her love language was food; she made sure I was fed well at all times, if I was sad she would take me to McDonald's or make me whatever lunch I wanted.

The next love I knew, was from my mom, but she was not the emotional type. There was never a hug or space for an emotional connection. She was either at work, at school or sleeping. Now don't get me wrong, she was a great mom but her emotional love capacity just was not there. I remember her love language being shopping; when I did good in school or did well with my chores she would reward me by taking me shopping. So that told me love equals money...

Growing up without my biological Dad, I was never taught what love was from a father-daughter perspective. "They"

20

(and I use the word "they" loosely) say a girl's first love is her dad, however my first love was my abuser. At 11 years old I felt what I thought at that time was love. He was the first person to tell me that I was beautiful, he was the first person to show interest in me for real. I remember when he and I first met, how he would always sit next to me and tell me how cute I was. That shortly changed once he found out how easy it was to manipulate me.

By the age of 12, I was determined that I wanted to know what love actually was! I figured I would have a baby, at least if I had a baby I would be loved by my baby, and my baby would never abandon me. I had no real clue what I was getting myself into, but I knew that I was yearning for something. I knew that I wanted to feel what this thing called *love* really was.

At the age of 13, I was pregnant, by the age of 14, I was a mother. No, my pregnancy was not an accident, I needed my son, I needed somebody to love and be loved by. When my son was born I had a different outlook on love, love meant nurturing, feeding, changing diapers, and to the best of my knowledge I was okay with that. However, six months into motherhood, I still was not fulfilled, I still felt unloved, I still felt like I needed more. This is when the promiscuity really kicked in. Maybe love is sex...... Or at least I was about to find out.

For years, I used men as toys, to fulfill my need for "love", which honestly, the sexual escapades only made me feel incomplete, sad, and used up. However, I continued, the more incomplete I felt the more men I would add to my rolodex of bed buddies. Sad... Yeah, I know now. Never knowing how depressed, lonely and sad I really was, I simply hid myself from myself. Yep, you read that right, instead of trying to heal my heart, I just kept going with what I knew to be the cure.

Let me paint the picture, as an early teen, I had three "boyfriends" ... But neither of them ever actually wanted to be with me for me. Each relationship, which was what we would call today a situationship or entanglement. In one relationship, I was being abused, mentally, emotionally and sometimes physically, but every day he swore that he loved me. The second relationship, he had other girlfriends, two of which hung in my circle in high school yet every day he, too, swore he loved me, he just didn't know how to be faithful to me. The third guy, I believe he just wanted somewhere to hang out at night and my house was where he would come because my mom worked nights. He didn't tell me he loved me but he was the one I spent the most time with, he was loving, never had a bad thing to say to me or about me. He was a really good friend, that happened to be a bed buddy. I lived this life ALL of my high school years and well into my 20's.

In my mid 20's I took the whole sex equals love up several notches by online dating, hanging out all times of the night, drinking heavily, smoking marijuana daily, making myself numb to all the hurt I was really feeling. I can remember not even recognizing the person that was looking at me in the mirror, I no longer knew who I was. By the time I was 30 years old I was in a deep depression but trying to live life as best as I could. On one hand, I knew what I was doing was wrong but on the other hand I didn't know what else to do. Like many others, when you don't know what to do you just do nothing. So, that's what I did...

By 35, I was at rock bottom, knowing that something had to change... Again, how to change, I had no clue..... In 2013, may have been early 2014, I tried to commit suicide; Thank God, HE sent my daughter to save my life. At that very moment my life changed. Not knowing what was happening, I moved to St. Louis, and started to find me.... Find me outside of the sexual desires, and wanting to be loved, I started to slowly unveil my true self. In 2015, I started my healing journey, I began therapy for all the childhood trauma, the domestic violence, and the sexual assault at the age of 8.... I began to truly peel off the hurt, layer by layer. In 2016, the mask came off, I wrote my first book and talked about being the Invisible Daughter. The healing that came with that release is indescribable. It was so powerful!!

Now at the age of 44, almost 45 (wow), I am so much better, I know that sex is not love by any means. I know that love is meant to heal you not hurt you. In order to know what love is, you must first love yourself. *"Well, Mikkita, how do I love myself and I don't know what it looks like?"* I am glad you asked... The bible is my go to... My prayer when I hit rock bottom was that God taught me how to love me for me, my prayer was that He begin to show me the real Mikkita and not the hurt person that I had become. The closer my relationship became with God the more I started to feel what love really was.

Life is amazing when you allow God to truly love on you. I look in the mirror daily and tell myself affirmations like.....

* You Are Amazing

* You are Love

* You Are ENOUGH

* You Are Healed

* You Are Loved

With telling myself these things I also read scriptures like:

Genesis 1:27: "So God created man in his own image, in the image of God he created him; male and female he created them."

Ephesians 2:10 ESV "For we are his workmanship, created in Christ Jesus for good works, which God prepared beforehand, that we should walk in them."

Psalm 139:14 ESV "I praise you, for I am fearfully and wonderfully made. Wonderful are your works; my soul knows it very well."

I am who God says I am... Anytime I feel lonely or vulnerable, I go to my Father and ask Him to hold me, to comfort me, to love on me just a little bit extra in that moment.

It is far from easy but every day I make the choice to live Whole, Happy, and Loved....

What does that look like? Well, I am happy that you asked.... It looks like me knowing who I am in God, knowing that every day may not be easy but every day is worth the challenges that it brings. It looks like making sure I have a therapist and use weekly therapy as needed. It looks like taking deep breaths when I get overwhelmed. It looks like me having self-care more than just going to get my hair done, or getting my nails done. It's about actually taking some me time outside of my children, outside of working, outside of being a Founder and CEO. I take time to simply be Mikkita, in whatever capacity I need at that time.

Healing me for me has been the most rewarding self-reflection I could have ever done. I don't take any of my traumas lightly and I will never tell anybody that I don't have any trials now that I am healing, but I will say I now have the tools to help me through them. Having the tools needed to get through everyday life is key to "living your best life".

I am Happy... I am WHOLE... I am Healing!!!!

I want to say to the readers of this anthology.... Take your time and read through the stories, read through the POWER of healing..... It has truly been an Awesome ride to victory!!!!

Chapter Two:

The Core of Loving Thyself

Antoinette B. Seawood

Antionette B. Seawood, a female entrepreneur & CEO of Naturally U'Nique LLC, U'Nique Getaways LLC & Be U'Nique Too Lashes. Such an innovator! Ms. Seawood aspires to become an international speaker, non-profit owner, and world traveler as a fashion stylist, worldwide.

Ms. Seawood, a former leader in manufacturing and logistics now speaks to the world through her brand while uplifting and encouraging those to step out of their comfort zone into their destiny. She believes that what you've been through can cause stagnation, but perseverance leads to freedom. Do you dare to be different?

This thought process was the first step toward Ms. Seawood getting out of her own way. Now she is an international author, the owner of 2 LLC's, a designer, a motivator, a speaker, a mental health advocate, and a kid at heart.

She speaks the following words while teaching others: *Find SERENITY and be who you were DESTINED to be! Be as TRANQUIL as the SEA, Rise, HOLD your HEAD High, grab ahold of those OBSTACLES & shine as bright as the SUN!! But in the midst of it all, Be U'Nique, Be YOU!*

As a leader in her entrepreneurial space, it brings her joy knowing that she is able to help change the lives of others who may be consumed with issues and fears they have so that they can move toward success. This passion ignited as she overcame her own life traumas which tried to destroy her. However, she survived. She currently chooses to use her life experiences to support others.

Lastly, Ms. Seawood speaks personal affirmations daily and encourages others to do the same. A few more are: Life isn't over, but it's what we make of it! Look in the mirror and stare yourself dead in the eyes and say, *those past traumas and heartbreaks will NOT break me! My time is NOW!* So, I say to YOU *Find SERENITY, keep pressing your way but, stay focused and DON'T forget to Be U'Nique and Getaway!* ***And Until Next Time,*** continue being the creator of your dreams and the main character of your success story.

The Core of Loving Thyself

Hey you, yes you! Let's chat about love really quickly! Love is learning to love who you are as a person! Being as though I was one of those women who believed ANYTHING that was told to me because I didn't love who I was and NEVER knew how, I looked to others to love me like I should've loved myself. Learning to love the skin that I was in from the inside out, from the deep tissue to the roughness of my skin. Learning to be intimate with myself as if I were in another shell and able to push those feelings of loving someone else unto myself. Caring about those feelings and being able to share them and not be embarrassed for loving who I am. I took time out for me to learn how to rise from what felt like death and gain new life as if I were a phoenix and be intimate with the person that I was forming into. I had to learn how to value myself, my person, my feelings, my emotions, my physical connections, and everything that came along with being me as a whole. Not knowing who I was, caused me to be insecure and very timid when it came to allowing people around me and in my space. I felt as if I wasn't good enough to be around. I felt like the entire world was better than the person I was created to be. When you learn to love who you are, it makes it easier for people to approach you, speak of you, speak to you and compliment you. When we have a lack of confidence it shows from the crown of our heads to the sole of our feet! When I learned to accept myself, my flaws, my bruises, and my scars, I was then able to allow the sun to shine down on me with stars that glared only on me! I placed myself in a different category and now I walk as if the world is mine with no worries. When I didn't know how to love myself as a person, I walked with my head down, feet twisted, crossing over one another because I wasn't confident enough to know that I could walk straight with my head held high as an ostrich. I always thought people was talking bad about me, I thought people were making fun of my disposition, how I moved, how I talked, just me being me. Love is being vulnerable to ourselves and knowing that we are allowed to expose our softer side and not always having to defend that softer side up against that rough side without feeling weak! I learned that it was okay to stand up, be seen, and be proud of who I am! I love myself more today than I did   yesterday & every day increases as I stand in the mirror and incorporate the importance of loving myself and my ability to now be courageous! I now share my truth with not just myself, but the world! Every day I take another step to push myself outside of what's comfortable to gain a new level of love for myself. I will never be perfect and I will allow myself to make mistakes without feeling as if I've done something tremendously wrong. I gave myself a break and I released all things that were toxic to retain my peace! Learning to love who you are is like getting a gold medal at the Olympics! You ran, you fought, you fell, you got back up, fell again, but you never stayed there after all the tussling and fighting trying to figure out who you were! Learning to love myself as a person made me want to love on every single soul that crossed my path because I wanted them to feel what I was feeling. I know what it's like to not feel loved, to be exempt, wanting to blow up just because someone looked at you. I never want people to feel how I felt. When I love I love hard, so learning how to love myself that way is absolutely amazing. I now wake up, look in the mirror and graze my hands across my face before I wash it, I smile at myself before I brush my teeth, I look at my figure and form before I take another step and realize that there is nothing wrong with me and what I see in that mirror is just what I was meant to be from head to toe, I love me just the way I am! Reflecting back in time, from my childhood, up until my life changed in 2019, I see that I never loved who I was. I learned to love who I was and how I created it to be authentic! I allowed people to mistreat me, talk bad about me, bully me, and not because I was afraid, but because, I was fearful that they would leave me and I felt as though I needed them. Learning to love who I am is the best thing I could've done to turn the tables in   my life. No telling how things would've turned out, because I had a bad attitude and I didn't like people. It took for me to shift my life and realize that the world hadn't done anything to me! The world wasn't to blame for my pain! The world was just the world and I was in it to live my life to the best of my ability and allow others to do the same instead of being hateful. Love is an amazing feeling when it's written in stone and the best love is self-love! If I hadn't learned to love who I am today, how could

I spread love to anyone else! At one point I became self-absorbed to give all the attention to myself and I felt I needed to be stubborn with what was mine. Love isn't an easy task and sometimes it takes away from others, but sometimes you have to put you first in order to retain or regain! We can't allow others to infiltrate our lives when we are trying to remain at peace, we have to be careful with how we allow others to handle us and invade our space! The love I have for myself today is like water in the ocean and even though my days aren't always calm, the love I have for myself outshines those rough days because it's always a beautiful ending, I love me today! My life is now like the ocean, my heart is filled with excitement. I inspire others and imagine what tomorrow will bring; not only for me, but for those connected to me and the joy I bring to the souls amongst me is like never before. To know that you can shine light on someone else without knowing it shows that your love shines deeper than just where you lay. When the waves in my life started to flow, I had to figure out the direction in which life was taking me. Love will lead you astray if you allow it, but the love I have for myself has taken over and I now allow that to motivate me to make the best decisions in life and one of them is moving forward. The high esteem that I have gained has allowed me to make decisions that will better nurture and serve me well. Finding a love that I never thought I'd find, because I never knew I'd lost It, has helped me put many pieces together from a puzzle that I'd been gathering for years. Loving who you are lessens stress and enhances your ability to focus and concentrate. I noticed all of these things returning slowly as I stepped back and allowed myself to heal from hurt and pain. This wasn't an easy process by any means, but it's definitely worth it! I had to separate myself from the world and shut everyone out; well not everyone, but the majority to focus on me. I had a guy friend that showed me daily that he loved me, but because I was lacking things in my life, I wasn't able to give it back 100%. Being loved and being able to give it back seems to be an amazing feeling, but when someone loves you and you can't reciprocate that same love, it's depressing because you haven't figured out the problem and you start to place blame and point fingers at everyone, but yourself! The life I have now is one I wouldn't trade to go backwards! I love every inch of my brown skin, my 4C hair, my love handles and even my chipped tooth. Learning to love me included the imperfections, bruises, and bumps! I am imperfectly perfect for me and all other love that's placed upon me just adds to the potion of love! I now strive to be the best version of myself and I will always run the race to beat the last best I performed for myself. In order to learn and perform self-love. I first had to sit down and ask myself how I felt, why I felt that way, and then try to rectify the things that were causing them. I then had to accept the why, when, and how to be able to think outside of the box as if I was an outsider with an opinion. Once those tasks were complete, I was then able to forgive myself for allowing the hurt, the abuse, the disrespect, and the toxic energy to take over my mind, my body, and my soul. I then learned how to say "NO" because at one point "NO" never came out of my mouth and I would bind myself just to say 'YES" so that people wouldn't' think bad of me. I learned how to deal with my tricky mind and beliefs before allowing them to take over and lead my mental capacity to an unknown place of disruption and dismantling. I want each of you to learn to love who you are as a whole and not partial. Don't allow others to predict your life, your love habits, your success, nor your presence when you enter a room! Learn to 'OWN" your movement, your feelings, your emotions, your stance, and anything that moves when you move! All of that comes with loving who you are full-fledged and not halfway, but entirely! Self-love leads to happiness, loving others authentically without force. Falling in love with you is like having love for a seed growing inside your womb! It's personal and very intimate and no-one should be allowed to disrupt that love because how we love ourselves allows others the opportunity to reciprocate that when they approach and step into our space. I use fashion to express just how much I love who I am today and that brings out the fierce, triumphant, robust, and courageous person that was hidden for years! I am now out and about, ready to show the world just how much love I have gained from the lessons learned and taught. Continue pressing your way to the top as you heal and learn to love who you are and all else will fall in line as it should. Leaves fall from trees and new ones grow! Flowers wither and die, but new ones bloom! We fall, but it's meant for us to get up and that's why we have hands and knees for assistance just in case it gets difficult to do alone. Use your knees to turn over and your hand to push yourself up, but whatever you do, get back up and try again! Love is learning to love ourselves so that we can learn to love others. Love is setting boundaries and learning to prioritize our lives, stick to commitments, strength and so much more. You know how they say talking to yourself isn't normal, well it is in my world, I do it on a daily. I look in the mirror and tell myself just how ahhhmazing I am as an individual. Just how proud I am of myself for taking everything that caused me hurt, pain and toxicity, and tossed it over my shoulders, and carried it with me as motivation to keep moving and continue to increase the love I had gained for myself! I want each of you to keep loving on you no matter the storm. Life will never be perfect and it was never meant to be but take it as it is and use it as a stepping stone to what lies ahead. Love thyself and thyself will learn to love others!

Chapter Three:

You Can't Teach What You Don't Know

Nikita Nicole

Nikita Nicole

#GodsGirl #TheHoodsGirl

Is a visionary who has set out to encourage, engage, equip, transform, and inspire those who find themselves trying to navigate through trials, tribulations, and traumas of life in a safe, healthy, and productive way. This midwife of intentionality helps people give birth to an intentional and obtainable plan for a positive and product future; through using two methods she created; The Push, Pray Proceed Method, as well as The BeIntentional Method. Both which have allowed her to not only flourish, while protecting her peace; but acknowledge, destroy, and rebuild her moral, spiritual, and mental foundation for a better life.

You Cannot Teach What You Don't Know

Sitting by myself I began to reflect on my life wondering, *'How did I end up here? Pregnant at 32 by I man I do not even like let alone want to have a baby with. Why am I not settled in my life? Why am I surrounded by people that do not value who I am? I am a good person; I have a good heart. I give and I give, and I give until I am depleted.'*

That was when a light bulb went off that something was not adding up and it was time for me to do some work on self. I did not feel right. There would be times when I was surrounded by people and felt so alone. I knew this was not love. I knew love was not supposed to make you sad.

The first thing I decided to do was to evaluate my life. What did all these people have in common? Me, of course! So, it was fair to say I was the problem, but how? That was what I was determined to find out.

First thing I did was began to look at my life growing up with my family, primarily my grandmother, seeing that she raised me. I realized that my grandmother was not a very emotional person. She did not talk about feelings and things of that nature. She was big on providing and making sure that our needs were met at a financial level. I realized over time that because she came from nothing, being financially stable was how she showed love (providing for you). We did not talk about emotions and how to manage them, nor did we talk about respect and boundaries regarding all type of relationships, even family. A lot of fundamental things I needed to know about how to interact with people in a healthy and correct manner was skipped, because she did not know. Over time I began to mimic bad behaviors (unfortunately) that I had seen growing up from the adults around me. Because they were adults, I believed it to be okay. But now my mind was different and what I wanted for me and this third and last child is changing.

I was pregnant with my third child at thirty-two years old when I realized that I had no real understanding of who I was; what I wanted; or what I was really doing in this thing called life. The way I loved was based on what I had seen, but I had no real conversation about what love was. As I began to be around and witness relationships that other people had, I realized there were some core principles that I was missing.

While I was trying to figure out what I was experiencing emotionally at the time, I had a few friends who were attending a neighborhood church and kept hounding me to attend. Finally, one Sunday in the summer of 2011 I took them up on the offer. I had no idea that this encounter would change my life forever. When I first started attending church, I was just a body in a building. I was not inspired at all. The best way to describe me at that time was by using the words bland and unmoved; I had a very still attitude and my demeanor was not very inviting.

How could it be, I was battling so much mental warfare I could not be open to anything else. But I remember the day a member of the choir sang, 'I know I've been changed' and in that moment those words spoke to, not where I was but where I wanted to be. I remember instantly being moved at 8 months pregnant. I had on blue, six-inch heels, and realized that I had no real control over what my body was doing at that moment; this was my first encounter with God in the form of the Holy Ghost. Leaving church that day with a feeling that there was more to life than what I was doing. That I deserved more. And that while I was genuinely excited about bringing my daughter into this world, I still felt empty inside. The desire to feel authentically happy was so much bigger than me, and I knew that it would require a different type of effort from me to achieve it. While church was the foundation in which it started, I sought out a licensed therapist because I did not know where to start, and I hoped they would give me some clarity.

Now Comes the Work

Walking into the therapist office I remember being absolutely uncomfortable and out of my element. In my family we did not see therapists.

"So, Nikita, what brings you in?"

I twist in my seat as if I had no reason to be there at all.

"Okay, let's start off with this question, are you crazy?" the therapist says.

Instantly, I get offended. "No, I am not crazy, are you crazy?"

"Okay, well if you don't think you're crazy, what are you feeling?"

"I do not know. I am trying to figure some things out and I feel like I cannot do it on my own, so…"

"Okay what are you trying to figure out?"

Me looking crazy.

"We can sit here all day, but you will not get anything from it, and you will still end up paying. Now, are you trying to waste your money, or do you want to do some work?"

I instantly began to talk; I like when people are direct with their approach to me. "I am pregnant, and I hate the father. Okay, I do not hate him, but I definitely would not have picked him for my baby. And I am starting to see a pattern."

"Okay, you said a pattern, well what pattern do you think you're seeing?"

As I began to peel away all the things from my adulthood, I realized that since the time I was able to date I had never been alone. The first real disappointment was the failing of my first marriage (which should have never happened).

But because I did not know how to be alone before my marriage was fully over, I had started another relationship. Mostly because I just wanted to feel special and wanted. I assumed that it was going to make me feel better. Which it did temporarily.

My therapist asked me "What does love look like to you?" This question confused the heck out of me because I did not know. I promised myself if I were going to be here, I would be honest, so I told her the truth.

"Ummm, I do not know. I guess a person being there for you when things go bad. Having your back if you get into a situation."

"So based on what you just said if you call me in the middle of the night and I come help you out does that necessarily mean I love you or that I'm just a nice person?"

Once again, I am stumped because I never thought of that. "I guess you could just be a nice person.," I responded.

As I continued to go to therapy and really work on me, I started to realize that no one can love you more than you love you. And the way you love you, teaches people who enter or are in your life how to love you.

During this time, I found that boundaries were a massive thing for me. Once I mastered boundaries, a lot of things fixed themselves. However, setting them was a problem for me. Boundaries can show up in many different ways. For instance, not giving people full access at their convenience, because they need you at that moment. It could be limiting the places you attend. Believe it or not sometimes it has to be boundaries on the type of conversations you have and with whom you have them with. When you set boundaries, it gives a clear-cut set of rules for what you will and will not accept as it pertains to you. This only comes when you really begin to understand self. Pay attention to your mood after doing and discussing certain things. Listen to your gut! But with boundaries there must be consequences. Telling someone not to do something and then ignoring the behavior once they do it defeats the purpose. The consequences do not have to be immediate termination from your life, but maybe you will change how you deal with them for a little while or deny them as much access to you.

The next thing I had to learn was the power in my NO! If we are not careful the inability to say No will leave us overwhelmed and frustrated. Even in some cases, resentful. You become overwhelmed because you take on way too much. For example, when asked to do something and you say No, but you do not stick with it, or you say yes when you really want to say no. After time it will began to frustrate you. Resentment sets in because you do not understand why they would ask you in the first place, and now you have an attitude. But if you find your No, what it will do is; allow you to only take on things you want to and can afford to do without a breakdown. It keeps your mental in a good place because you are not stressed. More importantly your No will allow you to see the people in your life and the respect and love they have for you. No one likes to be told No but people who authentically love you will respect it.

I had to learn to be okay with my own company. This is something that is so important but very few have mastered. The ability to be by yourself and not feel less than because of it. The complete feeling that if I do not have anyone with me IT'S OKAY. A lot of times we are either in a relationship, have kids to care for, a group of friends to hang with, or endless things we sign ourselves up for just to avoid the one-on-one time with self. But again, once you become comfortable with self, Setting Boundaries and Using your NO becomes so much easier to do.

Lastly, I started speaking a language to myself that I had never spoken before. The language of love. I became remarkably familiar with affirmations as I began to understand that if I affirmed myself, I would not look for or need anyone else to do so. Affirmation only works if you believe in them. My affirmations brought about my manifestation. You must speak to where you are now as well as to where you want to be. Then operate as if it is already happening. I even have affirmations that helps me remember how far I have come in case I forget. They are personal for me. Currently, I had the idea to combine the holiday I love most which is Christmas and affirmations; so, I created an affirmation tree. I took plain ornaments and wrote affirmations all over them and put them on the tree that is in my room. I needed to see and say them on a regular. After a while they became embedded in my mind. *Side note: This is also perfect if you are trying to reverse years of negative thinking or self-sabotage.* As I started affirming myself, I no longer had the energy to be around anyone who did not treat me well.

The more I learned how to properly love me the easier it became to put me first. The more I put me first and managed me in the right manner; those that genuinely loved me respected the changes and began to move accordingly. I began to align with what my true purpose was. What changed the most for me was I began to realize that relationships that I once thought I had been not relationships at all, but actually trauma bonds. These people were connected to me because they were able to see the emptiness or lack of love within me and they rested there. We were united not from love of one another; but from love of the same dysfunctional traits, we had or traumas we experienced. As I healed and began to love me it made them feel uncomfortable. I set the boundaries, so our conversations and my accessibility began to change. I started using my No, so we did not do the same things anymore. And because I was comfortable being alone, I was not willing to revert just to have people around me. I did not need to tell them to leave, when they started to receive this new energy, they decided to leave on their own. I did not make an announcement; I just simply decided to love me and to show up as the best version possible each and every day.

Life happens and you cannot always choose how people see you or value you. What matters the most is how you see and value you and that you stay true to that. Remove any thing or any person that tries to alter or derail that. Walk in your truth and do not apologize for doing what is best for you. Understand that even with doing all of this we are human so sometimes people in your life will make mistakes and that is okay. I am not saying your interactions with people will become perfect. What I will say is once you have started doing these things being loved and loving in a healthy manner will sure circle all around you. Even in the mist of the disagreement.

The Power of... What Is Love??

Chapter Four:

To Be Loved! Oh, What A Feeling... To Be Loved!

Francesca Cole-Barnes

Francesca Cole-Barnes, a Licensed Clinical Professional Counselor, is the founder and Lead Clinician at Faith Changes Behavior. This counseling practice specializes in Psychodynamic Psychotherapy, Trauma-informed Psychotherapy, and Child-Parent Psychotherapy. Francesca has nearly 12 years of clinical experience working with individuals, couples, families, parents, and children in various settings, including schools, home-based services, and community centers. Francesca also provides faith-based services to those who desire religious practices incorporated into their treatment.

Francesca is currently a 2nd-year doctoral student at The Institute for Clinical Social Work, where she aspires to obtain her Ph.D. in Clinical Social Work.

Francesca is also a self-published author of "The Elephant in the Room,"; a child-friendly book designed to help parents talk with their child or children about the birth of a new baby.

To be loved!
Oh, what a feeling to be loved!

Many of us are familiar with the famous scene from the 1988 hit movie "Coming to America," when Prince Akeem (played by Eddie Murphy) sang loudly on a New York street in Queens about what a feeling it was to be loved. This singing number followed Prince Akeem's date with his love interest Lisa (played by Shari Headley), whom he aspired to marry and make the queen of his homeland, Zamunda. Prince Akeem felt he had finally found the woman of his dreams and wanted the whole world to know, no matter how much they disapproved of his singing.

But is the definition of love professing it as loudly as possible so that everyone around you knows? Is love defined as finding that special someone who makes you do the darndest things, like embarrass yourself without remorse? Or is love a feeling, an experience, or something you know innately? I believe love is all the above and so much more.

The Oxford Dictionary defines love as an "intense feeling of deep affection; a great interest and pleasure in something." (Oxford, 2022) One of my favorite books, "The 5 Love Languages", describes love as a "confusing word" (Chapman, 2010, p. 19) and as a word that we use "in a thousand ways" (Chapman, 2010, p. 19). And according to 1 Corinthians 13:1-7, love is patient and kind. Love is not jealous or boastful or proud or rude. It does not demand its own way. It is not irritable, and it keeps no record of being wronged. It does not rejoice about injustice but rejoices whenever the truth wins out. Love never gives up, never loses faith, is always hopeful, and endures through every circumstance." (NLT Version)

So, according to the above sources, love is loud, it makes us behave a particular way, and it is what we feel. Love is multifaceted, such as the love of a person, a pet, an activity, or an object. Depending upon the relationship, such as love towards a child, it can be innate. Love is deep, a form of affection, and it takes time. We do not hold love over someone's head as a form of control, and love is not about who is right or wrong. Love should never give up easily, yet it should be enduring and everlasting.

As I begin to speak briefly about 'what is love,' I want to share my experience of love from early childhood, as a parent, and from a romantic perspective.

I grew up with parents who affectionately expressed love to me as a child. My mom had four children and always made time to show love physically and audibly. My mother's embrace meant she wanted us close to her ~~and~~ as though she never wanted to let go. Her kisses symbolized how we carried her love around with us and that there were more to come. Her verbalization of love was similar to hearing your favorite song on repeat that never wore out. I experienced my father's love through his words of affirmation. My father was my number one fan and always expressed how proud I made him. My father encouraged me to dream big and celebrated every one of my accomplishments as though it was my first. Even when my father and I were apart for a brief time in my life, his love found its way back to me as if it had never left. To this day, I am the apple of my father's eyes, and his love reminds the little girl in me and the woman I am today that we are loved.

Receiving unconditional love from my parents provided me with a baseline of how I should experience, express, and internalize love. I saw love and felt its presence whenever I wanted or needed it and learned at an early age that my parents' love was not the result of my 'good' behavior or 'good' grades. My parents wanted me to know that they loved me simply because I was their child and that I was deserving of their love for that very reason. I never felt the need to do anything for their love other than be myself.

I internalized my parents' unconditional love and sought to replicate it throughout my teenage, young adult, and adult years. The internalization of their love meant I believed it to be the most natural exchange of affection from one person to the next. I imagined it was how other parents expressed love to their children and in romantic relationships. Unfortunately, this would not be the case nor my experience when I entered my first long-term relationship. I did not experience love with my then partner as I had from my parents, and the meaning of love also seemed to change. Love felt strange, unavailable, and conditional. Love was not mutual and hurt more times than not. And when love started to come alive in the relationship, it would crash and burn a short time later. I began to ask myself, *What transpired that love became something I dreaded rather than something I wanted to feel? Why did I want to run away from 'this' kind of love and never look back?* I wondered if I was experiencing the 'wrong' type of love and whether what I had once known was still possible. No matter what love was trying to convince me to believe at this stage in my life, I refused to believe it and never gave up hope that I would experience 'my' kind of love again.

Shortly after ending that long-term relationship, I came face to face with a different kind of love, a love that resembled my parents' yet was more powerful. A love that made me smile as though I was in a teenage love story. A love that made me laugh tears. A love that produced butterflies in my stomach and had me walking on Cloud 9. A love that God whispered to me He tailored me for me and a love He spoke longevity over. A love that God joined together and commanded to let no one separate. A love between my husband and me.

Before I share what love is between my spouse and me, I want to talk about what love is for me as a mother of four children.

Having my first child at 17 was challenging. I was not mentally, emotionally, or financially prepared to care for another being and wondered how successful I would be as a young mother. And while I was concerned about the future of our well-being, the love I had for my daughter was innate. The moment the doctor laid her on my chest, I immediately felt love for her. I never wanted her out of my sight and was protective of her. My daughter was my sole responsibility, and I wanted to prove to us that I could provide her with the love she needed and deserved. Having a child also meant I could pass along to her the experiences I had with my parents in hopes of her doing the same for her children one day. As a result of loving my daughter, I gained confidence I could love my son once he was born, and loving my son made it easier to love my two youngest daughters.

The expression of love between my children and I is similar to my early experience with my parents. We physically hug and kiss each other and enjoy being near one another. We regularly verbalize our love and send "I love you" messages throughout the day. Mentally and emotionally, we love each other by creating space in our minds and hearts for one another, and we spiritually lift each other in prayer. And as my children mature in life, so has my love for them. I have learned the significance of having a different type of love for my adult children than I have for my two adolescent daughters. While I do not love one child more or less than the other, I acknowledge the love for my adult children means I am more supportive of their positions in life and use my love as a guide to how I show up. My love is patient with their walk in life and is sometimes quiet as they figure out their God-given paths. As for my youngest children, my love is stern to prevent them from following the wrong crowds. My love listens to their thoughts and opinions and assists us with finding a solution that works best for all. My love can also be quiet as they learn to problem-solve and build autonomy. Loving my children has been one of God's greatest gifts, next to loving my husband.

Love with my husband starts with our love for God, respect for one another, consistent communication, and intimacy.

When my husband and I began dating, we sought to build our love relationship on a God-first foundation. We discussed God's Word together, prayed together, and eventually worshiped together in the same church home. I must admit that my relationship with God deepened during the season of dating my husband. Witnessing his knowledge and love for God challenged me to do the same. Our increased hunger and thirst for God significantly impacted our relationship with the Lord, with each other, and individually. God's influence led us to take a two-month break from dating to seek the His face about the trajectory of our relationship. Our two-month journey of alone time with God strengthened our relationship with the Lord and reminded us that He ***always*** needed to be at the head of our relationship. You can say we were getting a jumpstart on making God a part of our cord of three strands. And after nearly 12 years of marriage and almost 16 years of dating, God remains and will continue to reside at the center of our love story.

Out of our love for God, there grew respect for one another. Respect as a form of love means we regard each other in public and within the privacy of our home. My husband and I do not seek to show each other up, nor do we feel the need to prove who is in charge of our relationship. We acknowledge, understand, and esteem the many roles we play, which can change depending upon the day of the week. We value what we each bring to the table and do not frown upon if one of us is ever short because we know it is about equal sacrifice rather than equal giving.

Respect leads to us desiring consistent communication in our relationship. Our constant contact limits assumptions or misunderstandings and encourages straightforwardness. Verbally communicating as a form of love means holding a position to speak our truth and listening to the other's truth, whether or not we agree. It means discussing household decisions, phone calls throughout the day, or non-verbally communicating by texting each other love songs.

And then there is intimacy. Intimacy is a significant love language in my marriage, and my husband and I equally invest in it as we do everything else to keep our relationship healthy. While sexual intimacy is paramount in a committed relationship, intimacy between my husband and I, means talking and laughing for hours after our children are in bed. It involves gazing and smiling at each other when we least expect it or holding hands as we fall asleep. No matter the expression of our intimacy, the goal is to keep it alive for the duration of our marriage.

As I return to Prince Akeem's scene of him openly expressing his love for Lisa, to be loved from a personal and therapeutic perspective means mentally, emotionally, and physically creating space for love. One means of creating space is internalizing love from positive early childhood experiences. Because our parents are our first point of contact regarding what love looks and feels like, it is salient for those early experiences to be a guide for the expression of love when we are no longer within the parental environment. To be loved also means believing there is a God-given person tailored-made just for you. That God-given person can be a child, a romantic partner, or perhaps a friend. Through these relationships, we can be playful and creative with how we express and receive love, and these relationships provide us with the opportunity to expand our capacity for love.

Chapter Five:

Unconditional Love

Timothia Reid

 Educator, book lover, and new author **Timothia Reid** is passionate about pretty much anything in print and improving the quality of life of children in her community. She has over 10 years of experience in the education field where she has worn many hats; such as teacher's aide, substitute teacher, Title 1 aide, and classroom teacher. She has an Associate's degree in Early Childhood Education, a Bachelor's degree in Psychology, and a Master's degree in Education with a concentration in Reading Literacy. Timothia is a CASA (Court Appointed Special Advocate) in her county where she helps check in on children and families within the foster care system. She is on the Black Advisory Board and the 4th Grade Scholastic News Magazine Advisory Board for Scholastic where she shares her passion for books by providing teachers and students with resources that will improve the quality of literacy in classrooms. She is also a speaker on the Art of Transparency Tour where she shares her story with those who are willing to listen and learn. Timothia currently lives in Illinois with her two children and in her free time she loves to spend time with them, read books, and enjoy life to the fullest. She has even ventured into acting in plays recently.

Unconditional Love

I Never Knew Love

I never knew love until I felt you move and stretch in my inner core.

I never knew love until I looked into your eyes and heard you cry for the very first time.

I never knew love until my fingers tenderly touched your skin as I cradled you on my chest so you could listen to my heartbeat.

I never knew love until you smiled up at me and made me laugh during life's crazy, tough times.

I never knew love until you said my most favorite words..."I love you" and "You're the best".

I never knew love until I felt you hug me so tight from the fear that I would let go and never come back.

I never knew love until you were sick and I was scared of losing you on that dark, scary, and lonely night.

I never knew love until you came into my life and made me whole.

My angels. My blessings. My motivation. My reasons for living.

I never knew love until I was blessed with the two of you.

Timothia Reid, 2022

I've known love from the very moment that I knew myself. I never doubted in my mind that there would always be that one person who would always love me and would be there for me, my mom. You see, from day one she sacrificed and put us first. For years I never understood the reasons why she did some of the things she did for me, but now as an adult I understand her more day after day. Believe me when I say that I have given her more than enough reasons to wash her hands off of me, turn her back, and walk away. However, my angel is always there to pick me up, dust me off, pray me back up, and send me on my way. Of course, the long lectures never failed to accompany all of this, but as I listen to her wisdom I know that most of the time she is right. We don't always agree on everything but we listen to each other. I never got to know my biological father. My only memory of him was hidden behind a nightmare that I had for years as a child. I was lost in a building trying to find him, trying to find anyone. I had somehow lost my way. There was also a gun that came out of nowhere. This nightmare haunted me through my childhood and teenage years until one day as an adult I finally told my mom about it. I don't know why I never shared this with her, but when I did, she then explained to me that it wasn't a dream after all but a mere suppressed memory. The memory came from a time when I spent the day with my father. I got lost and we were robbed at gunpoint. After that, I never had that nightmare again. I did have a male role model in my life, my stepdad, who essentially stepped into my father's shoes very early on in my life. He has been the only father I have truly known. He was and continues to be a great provider but his knowledge of parenting ended there. As long as there was a roof over our heads, food on the table, and money in the bank to pay the bills; he really thought that was all it took to raise children. I can't really blame him. That's all he knew. Our relationship was not the best, especially during my teenage years. To be honest, there were years when I thought I hated him and would never forgive him for things he did. Today, however, our relationship is growing and I'm proud to call him my dad. I never heard him tell me "I love you" while I was growing up, but hearing it now as an adult has filled a gap in my heart that I never even realized existed to begin with.

I thought that my mom's love was the purest form of love that I would ever know. I thought that no one could love me as unconditionally as she could. I thought that I would never love anyone as much as I love her. She is my anchor when I am all over the place and feel like I've lost my way. She is my cheerleader when I give up on myself. She is my air supply when the world sucks out every breath from my body and soul. While she is still all of these things and more in my life today, a new facet of parental love would come and change my life forever. Love took on a whole new meaning when I looked into my children's eyes for the very first time.

Giving birth was one of the most intriguing and exhausting events I have ever experienced. It is one of the most painful things you could probably feel as a woman but that pain seems to just fade away the very moment you look into the sweet face of your baby. It's like you forget that you were in loads of pain just mere seconds before looking into those sweet baby eyes. The instant love that I felt when I held them for the first time cannot even be described. My husband was with me during the birth of our son and he was with me during the loss of our second child, but he had passed away in a car accident earlier in the year when I was pregnant with our daughter. Giving birth by myself was the loneliest feeling I have ever felt. However, once I held her in my arms for the very first time, I knew that everything would be okay even though I knew the journey ahead would not be easy. I often wonder about our second child and what he or she would have been like. I found out early on during that pregnancy that it was an ectopic pregnancy. My baby was stuck in one of my Fallopian tubes. One tube along with the pregnancy had to be removed or I could have lost my life as well. But God...

Both of my kids were in a hurry to get here so my mom missed both of their births. Having her there to help me once she arrived meant the world to me, especially after the first one. I had no idea what to do with this baby! It just kept peeing everywhere, pooping all the time, and drinking up all of my breast milk like it wasn't enough! The second time around I simply surrendered my baby girl to her when she arrived and went to bed. You see, we were sent home earlier that week but she would not arrive until the next weekend. That week was a blur because my son was only 2 years old and slept through the night, but my newborn was sleeping through the day. I didn't sleep at all for about a week. I'm not kidding! That week was a complete blur in survival mode until she got there to help me. Eventually, I got the hang of it. I remember promising myself and my kids that I would be the best mom I could possibly be for them. Did I make mistakes? Of course! What parent doesn't? I simply tried to learn from them and moved on. At one point in my parenting journey I felt the need to find a suitable father figure for my children. Boy, was that a disaster! I'm still not an expert in that field of love and recently realized that I have done and am doing a great job raising my children on my own.

According to the Encyclopedia Britannica, parenting is the process of raising children and providing them with protection and care in order to ensure healthy development into adulthood. Many people think that raising children ends when they turn 18 years of age. I was one of those people at one point. I had them at a young age so I had my plans set that they would be grown and out of the house by the time I turned 40. Boy, was I wrong! I think I worry about them more now as adults than when they were kids. Now I get to teach them the adult side of life and guide them as much as they will allow me to. It's hard thinking about life without them around the house playing or yelling at each other while eating up all the food and creating messes all over the house. It's scary to think that soon my house will be silent without them in it. I know it's a part of life and I'm learning to accept it. I'm learning to be "just me" again. For so long I have put their needs before mine that I have now had to face the reality that I lived most of my life for them. I don't regret any of it and I would do it again in a heartbeat. If they only knew that having them changed my life forever and I have become the woman that I am today because of them.

After having my daughter, I decided to go to college. I had friends who tried to talk me out of it because they thought I needed to focus solely on my children now that their father had passed away. At that point I made a promise to myself that my children's well-being would always come first but that I also needed to get an education in order to provide them with a comfortable life. As a parent we make sacrifices for our children. Spending time with them has always been my number one priority. I never wanted them to feel like anything was more important to me than them. If an activity did not allow for me to bring my children with me, then I would not attend. If you saw me, you saw them. They went everywhere with me because that was important to me. For that reason I chose a community college that had a daycare in it where I could work part-time and see my children throughout the day. Oftentimes, seeing them through the one-way glass was a well-needed motivator on days when I felt like giving up. Next, I chose to go to school online to earn my bachelor's degree when it was not the popular thing to do back then. Making that choice meant that I would be home every night with my children. There were plenty of long days but I did what I felt I needed to do for the well-being of my children.

Life has taught me many lessons but the one that I treasure the most is that your children are always watching everything that you do and listening to everything that you say. Oftentimes it felt like their selective hearing would kick in more often than not, but then they would do or say something that would remind me of what I have taught them. It's funny to hear them talk about how I raised them and how their stories sound very different from what I actually remember happening, if I remember the event at all! They often say how they will raise their children the same way. I'm not sure if that's a compliment or if I should be worried! It does however show me that they think highly of me and what we have accomplished as a family. I know they are going to make mistakes throughout their lives and I truly hope that they know they can always count on me; just like I can always count on my mom. Being a parent is not an easy task. If it was, everyone would be great at it and we would not have all the trauma that kids go through daily. Having children taught me that life was not just about me anymore. I had two precious souls to take care of and protect. I learned that sometimes getting the things that you want for yourself may have to wait or you may have to find a different route to achieve those lifelong dreams. I learned that I could do anything because I had them and because I knew that they were looking up to me. I knew that if I gave up on life, I would be letting them down also. I learned that when you take the time to plant good things in your children, they will grow up and hopefully continue to spread good vibes and sunshine into this dark, cruel world. If my kids only knew how proud I am of the man and woman they are becoming, they would understand that I love them unconditionally and that I am here whenever they need me.

Chapter Six:

Love Is the Greatest Gift

Morgana Matthews

Pastor Morgana Matthews

Born and raised on the south-side of Chicago a mother of four beautiful daughters. I Was introduced to the Lord at a young age but it didn't become real to me until my early twenties. Following my mother, I Moved to Milwaukee where I began to hear from the Lord regarding the mantle He has on my life. He began to unfold His Word to me and showed me in John 12:32 that if He be lifted up from the earth, He would draw all men unto HIM. Under the leadership of Apostle Lock Sr. I began to evangelize and spread the Word, lifting up the name of Jesus and drawing souls to glorify the kingdom of God. Under the leadership of the bishop Burt, I was the lead over the outreach ministry, I taught and preached there for five years. Under the leadership of bishop Oilphant I was Pastor of outreach, Sunday school teacher, and served on the hospitality team. As a visionary and Bible teacher, preacher, author, and Conference speaker. I continue to serve God in my own ministry which is Sent by God outreach ministries. I Continue to serve the people as God serves me. I believe Numbers 23:19 that says God is not a man, that He should lie; neither the son of man, that He should repent: Hath He said, and shall He not do it? Or hath he spoken, and shall He not make it good? As I travel, I continue to seek God for what He is doing in this season for His people and preaching and teaching God's Holy Word wherever I go.

Love Is the Greatest Gift

To answer the question right off the bat, God is love and I am going to prove that to you. To know real love, we must be born again, which means to accept Jesus Christ as your Lord and Savior and commit your life to Him. It is only after we have done that, that we will experience real, pure, and genuine love. Until we experience the love of God for ourselves; we will never be able to express it to others. You cannot give what you do not have. Everything changed for me when I found out how much God loved me. His love was not predicated or contingent on anything I did. He showed His great love toward me because He is love. Love is not just an attribute {a quality or character}; love is who God is. John 3:16 says for God so loved the world that He gave his only begotten son, that whosoever believes in him should not perish but have everlasting life. A few take-a-ways here: love causes you to give, it causes you to do something. Love is a verb, which means action, not lip service but action. God gave his only son [action]. This tells you and me that love is not about a feeling but a doing. This love I am talking about is divine. There are four Greek words regarding love that we will look to further understand what love is. Agape is used to speak of God's love he has for the world and that Christians are supposed to emulate. This love is unconditional, sacrificial, and selfless. As humans, we think we know what real love is, but we do not. Human or natural love can only be given and felt or received when our conditions or needs are meet. Romans 5:8 says but God commended his love towards us, in that while we were yet sinners; Christ died for us. I do not know many people who will die for you who say they love you; I certainly do not think that anyone would die for you if you were estranged from them. However, Jesus did!! The other Greek word for love is eros, which refers to romantic or sexual love, from this word we get the word erotic. How many times have we given ourselves to people in a sexual way and thought we were loved? Sex and lust are two words that do not have to be connected to love. You can have sex with someone and not love them. Lust is having a strong desire for sex, a craving, or appetite. A lot of times two broken people come together and produce broken children out of lust trying to fill a void that only God can fill. We all want love and companionship, but it must be real and true. Letting someone use your body as a drive-thru is not love. Love is all about commitment and honesty. The other Greek word for love is storage, which refers to familial love like that a mother has for her baby or love between a brother or sister.

I believe after the love of God the next purest form of love is that of a mother and her child. You carry that little one in your womb for nine months. This is an unbreakable bond; you do what you must to make sure that your baby is taken care of, and you are present. It is hard to love from a distance. Love will always cost you something, that is not a terrible thing. If whatever you are a part of or connected to does not cost you anything then it is not important. The other Greek word for love is Philia, this refers to friendship and camaraderie. This word is translated as the love you will have for a friend. The Bible says no greater love than this than a man lay down his life for his friend [John 15:13]. Real love causes you to do something, love is not passive. Love has quite a few attributes in nature; security, passion, compassion, dependability, support, reliability, trustworthiness, and most of all it is presence. Love feels good when it is authentic and pure. There is a quote from St. Augustine that says, "God loves each of us as if there were only one of us." We came in this world through sin and things became tainted. For us to get back to the way God planned it, we must get a new nature, and be born again. Before the fall of Adam and Eve, they were naked and not ashamed. They enjoyed each other without any problem. Our hearts need to be purified and open to give or receive love. 1 Corinthians 13 is considered the love chapter in the Bible. Let us look at some of the characteristics of love from this chapter; love is long-suffering, love is kind, love does not seek after its own, love is not puffed up, love is not easily provoked, love thinketh no evil, love beareth all things, believeth all things, hopeth all things, and endures all things. My God that is a great description of love and it comes right from the Word of God. If I had to give you a visual of love, face down it would be the picture of the cross. Love kept Jesus up on that cross. He could have come down, but he did not. He saw you and me and all those that would be saved by Him paying the ultimate sacrifice. The cross is vertical and horizontal, which means we must love God and man, but we cannot love without the Holy Spirit living inside of us. The Holy Spirit is our enabler. He helps us do things that on our own would be impossible. Let's keep it real, it is not easy to love some people. At times I am sure we can be hard to love but God expects us to love others the same way He loves you and me, unconditionally. None of us are perfect and we all need Grace sometimes when life pushes against us and we react in a way that does not bring Glory to God, I try to live my life with this thought in mind, God was patient with me, and I was a hot mess. He loved me right through all my mistakes and repeated offense. I know that is why I love Him so much. He never gave up on me even after all my mistakes. When a person feels loved and not judged they blossom like a beautiful flower. I know for sure that love is patient, it allows you to start over when necessary. If you fail at first, try again!! Love is too precious to give up on; we all need it, and we all want it. God surely set it up that way. I have come from a Spiritual point of view about love now let us gauge from a natural perspective what love looks like. Most of us growing up never saw love from our parent's relationship because chances are we grew up in a single-family home, Dad was gone and mom playing both roles. We grow up thinking sex and just having a man around is love. My heart breaks for Black children because they are exposed to too much negativity at an incredibly early age. Black people are brilliant people, but we allow what happened to us get in us and we go down a dark road. We began to emulate what we have seen and been exposed to, so we come in the world as far as love is concerned at a disadvantage. Our hearts become indifferent exceedingly early on. We learn to go along to get along in a lot of areas of our lives, we simply want to survive until we get old enough to try life for ourselves. So, we try life as adults, but we are broken from our childhood, we eventually become the thing we despised. For example, we did not like knowing our father or having a drug addicted mama because she has been pushed to the brink of playing two roles that she should not have to do. That is exactly what happens we do what we know and without any intervention the cycles repeat itself. This is the reason Black women are not loved, honored, and treasured as they should be. This is not a book about bashing races but instead a Black woman speaking from experience about why love eludes the worthiest woman on the planet, A Black woman. I do not know of a stronger woman in the world than a Black woman she wears twenty hats, and she does not let one fall. She works under conditions that others will fall under, she loves from a deep place, and she continues to give of herself for those she loves. She does it without expecting anything but respect and honor. To me that is love when you stick it out with someone no matter how you feel. Sometimes you do not feel in love, but it is at those times you stay true to your commitment to this person, or your children and you do what you know is right until your feelings catch up. The world that we live in now do does not honor those things that keeps families and communities strong. We must go back to Gods original plan and do things Gods way. Families are created from a man and a woman period. Two women cannot have children together and neither can two men. This spirit of confusion has hit this land and people are doing all kinds of things. You cannot do wrong and expect right to be your answer. You cannot go against the Word of God and think life is going to be good. If we want to see things turn around in our land, we must repent and seek God's forgiveness for the mess we have made by not being obedient to Him and His Word. The Bible says there is a way that seems right to man but at the end there is death. Without the leading of the Holy Spirit, we do not have a clue as to what we should be doing. Go back and read your bibles God did not set it up from the beginning for us to be in this state, God had a perfect paradise for us, we walked around naked and unashamed. We were in fellowship with the Creator of the universe, but sin entered in through sin and the first Adam. God created us a little lower than the angels and He gave us a will to choose. So, Adam and Eve allowed Satan to hood wink them to disobey God and All of the beauty they had that did not matter they wanted the one tree God told them not to eat from. Satan is using that same trick today making people feel like being a Christian is too hard or being a Christian is for lame people. I can promise you this if you give your life to Christ life will become bearable because God is with you no matter what you are going through, God is so faithful to His word. It is not how you start but how you end. Choose today whom you will serve, there is a Heaven and a hell. What you decide on this side determines where you will spend eternity when you die. You can choose smoking or known smoking. Heaven or hell do not be deceived and think this is all there is. We serve a king who will rule over a kingdom. I am still talking about love. Love is caring enough about a person where you speak truth to them. My prayer for you, Yes you that is reading this book that you will feel my Spirit and want to know one of the greatest Men I ever meet His name is Jesus, He gave His life for me and you and all He wants from me is to represent Him in a way that will cause others to do the same and come running saying what must I do to be saved. Someone said insanity is doing the same thing expecting a different response. You have tried things your way and it did not work out. Try Jesus and I am a witness He will never leave you nor forsake you. He will be whatever you need Him to be. Life is not as long as people think, and the only reason God has not returned yet is because He is giving people time to choose Him. The Bible talks about people hearts will become wax cold and how true that is, it is so much killing and people committing suicide at an all-time high, Mental illness is up there too.

The Power of... What Is Love??

We need God to help us navigate this life. I pray that something was written to point you to Jesus Christ, and I promise you whatever you need and whatever you are lacking fall in love with Jesus, and He will make life a lot more bearable because He is with you. Isaiah 26:3 Says those who keep their minds on Jesus, He will keep them in perfect peace. No matter what is going on around you when you have Jesus in you the joy of the Lord is your strength. Know this if you have not been loved on this side Jesus thought you were to die for. Think about that, Jesus died so that you and I can have fellowship with the Father, Which is love!! Lord, I pray that you Bless all that read this book, I pray that if they do not have a relationship with You, they will after reading about a Man who died for them and He did it because He loved them. I pray this Prayer in Jesus Mighty Name Amen. I love you all and that is why I wrote this chapter so that you would know you are loved, Respected, honored, and worthy to be loved. Love is Gods greatest gift to mankind, and He did it because He is love. When a person loves you for real they want to see you happy and flourishing, they are not looking to receive but to give. Love is a selfless act, you are always looking to Bless the other person, and in doing that you feel Blessed. I have truly been loved a few times in my life and I am telling you it is the most beautiful and fulfilling thing I have ever experienced. I have been loved by man and God and I am grateful for it. Keep your heart open and expect to be loved by God and by man you deserve to be cherished.

The Power of... What Is Love??

Chapter Seven:

Iridescent Kisses

Q. R. Williams

 Co-author, **Q.R. Williams** is an avid reader and book enthusiast. She is the owner of Epiphany Expression; a business that assists with creative writing and notary services.

She believes everyone should have access to adequate healthcare and treated with excellent customer service; which became the driving force behind her career path. She previously held the titles of: Care Navigator Supervisor, Senior Administrative Assistant and Client Service Professional. She is certified as a Community Health Worker and Mental Health First Aid Advocate. She is also certified in Restorative Justice 101.

Q.R. is also the co-author of the books 'After We Parted: Rebuilding Our Lives After Divorce', 'It's a Matron of Honor: Journey to Womanhood' & 'Because I Am More than Just My Skin'.

Family is very important to her. Q.R. is a newlywed; sharing her life with her husband, Joshua. She is also the mother of a teenage son, John.

I believe the Creator of the universe made all things, including the emotion, affection and action of LOVE. I thank YAH for all of the beauty it holds.

Let love and faithfulness never leave you... - Proverbs 3:3

"Let love reign; gifting you with an abundance of peace and joy."

Iridescent Kisses

There is a luxury mountain refuge; a colossal structure, but a place cozy enough to call home. As you enter, it's lucidly breathtaking. A cast iron fireplace sits in the corner of each main dwelling. It takes longer to heat up, but once it does you can be assured that it will provide enough warmth throughout the room. As the amount of popping and crackling increases from the firewood, this still feels like a safe spot to nestle. The logs slowly disintegrate, restoring the quietude. There are many windows wrapped around the atypical cabin. The amount of lighting and the outdoor view changes due to which window you gaze out of. The open concept designed by the architect provides a layout that gives amazing views, no matter the terrain. This complements the outdoor landscape. What you observe, depends on where you stand or at which angle you sit to survey the very thing right in front of you. You become an eccentric watchman over what is within your scope of visibility. Some windows are floor to ceiling, which naturally bridge the indoor timber with the outdoor greenery. Take a look by piercing out, intensely vetting the land abroad while somehow still wondering about the unseen, covered waters deep below. There is a sunray of hope that lingers above and days when multiple colors will fill the sky. The showing of luminous glow will eventually appear to shift, depending on your exact location. Your perception can greatly differ in each room, giving you a new outlook or experience. The unique hue can be described based on interpretation. What do you see?

Just like an iridescent sky, people can appear to change based on where they currently stand in their life's journey; reflecting on the things that have passed and meditating on the things that will be. We all go through cycles and that will also include misfortune. An interplay of multiple snapshots is greatly enhanced when they are kissed by a thing called love. What is love? You would receive a multitude of responses, depending on who you asked. Some people are still attempting to express what can be felt or visibly seen. Others may express that it is a void that has never been filled or an action that has never been learned. There are others who have witnessed it and its vulnerability, making an immense effort to avoid it like the plague. When a strong description of the word "like" overflows into much more, it becomes love.

One of the definitions of love states, "Love encompasses a range of strong and positive emotional and mental states, from the most sublime virtue or good habit; the deepest interpersonal affection to the simplest pleasure." [*reference, Wikipedia*]

I believe love can be so simple yet beautiful; serene like a dove. Oftentimes, it holds complexity in a unique way, like the combination of tinctures on a butterfly. I pray all are open enough to receive love and have the opportunity to embrace it, in its purest form. We all deserve to house love; share our space with love. It shouldn't be a forced command or uncontrollable emotions. It should not be caged around toxicity or controlled destruction. Yes, it is powerful but it should never be used to rule and belittle.

Love can be unconditional, yet it should not tolerate all things or be held hostage by even the inevitable.

As I pondered over the subject of love; I internally sketched a diagram in my mind. I call it the 'Love Trifecta'. It is a representation of three levels or areas of love. I believe love begins, first, when you are a recipient of it. It comes from a source that pours into you. I know we all have different belief systems, but most of us have faith that there is something greater than one's self that does exist. I believe that love initiates here. There are many thoughts, theories, and doctrines based on religion, spirituality, and naturalism. So much can be debated, proven, or debunked. Rather you describe it as God [Psalm 119:2, Proverbs 3:5-6], The Universe, or Mother Earth; When we feel connected to a Creator, The Most High, or feel like we are one with nature and affixed to science, that represents love and life. Now there is another very important piece to this that follows, it's you. There is an old saying, "You can't love anyone or anything unless you love yourself first". You can agree or disagree with that statement; I believe we all can agree or at least respect the idea that you should be able to find something within yourself that is lovable. Your makeup or your very existence should be pampered with love. You are a treasure filled with purpose, gifts, passion, talents, information, education, and career. That all can be recognized and cultivated by love; it should be embedded inside of you. This is not a braggadocious moment either, but I love me some me. I can say this as an affirmation with confidence. To be at this stage in life where I can encourage myself and be proud of where I stand. I can express with transparency, that there are improvements that need to occur without the demolition of my entire statuesque form. I am worth feeding not only my body, but my spirit plenty of goodness as well. My soul partakes in being adorned with iridescent jewels that cover me with love [Isaiah 61:10]. I am a work in progress, but I didn't get this far just to get this far. Greater is coming and I am loving who I am and more importantly, who I am becoming in the process. The last plank of this carries our relationships, commitments, and companionship. This is your tribe that may consist of a combination of your personal connection with others. It can be the covenant of marriage or parenting your children. Perhaps it's simply a village of family and friends; anyone of significance in your life. Those who make an impact and hold some merit. The way we categorize or encounter others help to establish how we care for them. What is in your heart and who has a place in your heart, represents the way that you love.

As I continue to visualize this Love Trifecta, it greatly reminds me of Divine Order. Who has your heart? I have discovered that we sometimes lend or give complete ownership of our heart to the wrong people. No individual should have complete control over your emotional motherboard. Don't make a single soul the chief operating officer of your heart. The heart in its physical form is said to be the hardest working muscle in the body. Don't give away all of your strength. In the wrong hands with a quick snip, you can be detached from it as Samson was when he divulged his secret to Delilah [Judges 16:15-20].

Continuously perform a heart check, disclosing the matters of the heart. Time will reveal how your love changes and who will receive all you have to offer within love. When you value something, you give it your time... your attention
...your love.

 Love is an emotional, reaction and a commitment. It is the choice to respond with care. It is a moment that you agree that feelings should be involved and it matters. Love can be a verb, displayed with action. Love is forgiveness or perhaps compromising at times, but it doesn't have to be accompanied by a constant tolerance. Love can be unconditional or dissolving; yes you can love from a distance. Everything you love won't be active in your life. Love should not be filled with anger or malicious behavior. Love goes beyond lust and infatuation. Love can lean towards foolishness for a moment, but never downright stupidity. When the blinders come off and you surpass having tunnel vision, something of substance should be in sight. When love ignites you don't have to tragically be burnt by its roaring flame. It doesn't have to be fueled by toxic traits, never letting you go while refusing to treat you right. It is not blunt trauma or uppercut punches of misery.

Love can be based on conditions or manifested when you speak its language. Love is powerful and bold. It is a pleasure when it is consistent and endearing. Love is smiles and laughter. Love is temperamental happiness or elongated joy. Love comes with a responsibility. We all have our different views on love and perceive it in our own way. Love is an emotion that correlates with movement. It is an act of physically expressing. Please remember to give love where it's appreciated and reciprocated.

There is a song by Bo Diddley, 'Who Do You Love?'. You should be able to honestly answer that. Love doesn't have to be this confusing thing, even though certain circumstances can complicate it. I am a self-proclaimed connoisseur of music. Music can express feelings when you may fail to utter the words; music can be the melody of love.

There is a powerful quote from Bob Marley that states, "The biggest coward of a man is to awaken the love of a woman without the intention of loving her." A man has found me, that has the valor and benevolence to love all of me; I have the moxie to receive those deposits and invest them back into the joined life that we share. It's finally genuine and refined; it's always enough. It's the crystallized sweetness near the honeycomb. It's the sap from the black maple tree. It's more than extended branches, but it's the love that springs up from the roots.

This is a breath of fresh air. This is a romanticized, rhapsodized love. I am now a witness that love is possible without continuous heartache and despair. Love feels like sunshine when it comes from the right people, at the right moment. Good Morning, Love! Thank you for finding me; waking me up with the phenomenal touch and greeting of Iridescent Kisses.

The Power of... What Is Love??

Chapter Eight:

Learning to Love Myself Better

Tonia Reaves

 **_Minister Tonia Reaves_**, also known as ToniaSurvives, is the Founder and CEO of Life Empowerment & Survival Ministries, a Domestic Violence Survivor Support Organization. She is a 17-year Domestic Violence Survivor and Advocate. She is the Founder of God's Safe Haven for Women & Children. She became a Licensed and Ordained Minister in November 2021. She is a Trained Prayer Intercessor, an Award-Winning Author, Kingdom Excellence Award 2021 recipient.

She co-authored in several Book Collaborations, such as "You Can, a Compilation of 33 Authors, "Essence of Her, a Study of Proverbs 31", "40 Days of Fuel", and currently working on an Anthology, "The Dealing With the Aftermath". Tonia is the Author of "My Butterfly Transformation, A Journaling Experience", released on October 29, 2021. She was an Honoree and Guest Speaker for the 2008 Sargeant Shriver Center on Poverty Law Annual Gala. She Testified in Springfield to Adopt VESSA Laws for State of Illinois Employees and Businesses Statewide after losing her job as an Illinois Employee due to taking an approved leave of absence because of Domestic Violence.

She received the "We Live and Dream In Color Humanitarian Award 2016". She is currently an Honoree for her work in Domestic Violence from the Better Sister & Brother Growth Network to be honored during their 2022 Annual Awards. She is an Award Winning Motivational Speaker and Spiritual Leader. She just recently joined The Art of Transparency Tour with Author Mikkita Moore and is working on a new Collaboration with Mikkita Moore's Invisible Daughter label, titled "What is Love?" Tonia is planning to start a journaling support group to begin April 8, 2022 for Survivors of Abuse.

Contact information: lifempowermentzone@gmail.com & toniasurvives@gmail.com Website: https://life-empowerment-survival.business.site

Learning How to Love Me Better

As I begin to write this chapter, I realize the title does represent me. I have not yet learned how to love myself better. I am being as transparent as I possibly can. When I look at myself, I see pain and past hurts that I can't seem to erase.

I can still hear the voice of my abusers saying the most hurtful and disrespectful things you could possibly think to say. The issue is, with abuser number one, I was only four years old when the abuse started. She was my babysitter. Her job was to make sure nothing happened to me or my siblings, feed us dinner, make sure we brush our teeth and bathed, then put us to bed. Instead, she chose to abuse me. She called me ugly, dumb, and stupid. She deprived me of dinner and physically abused me. She was the babysitter from hell. She kicked the wind out of me on several occasions. I almost always expected it on the nights my mom needed her to sit with us. I was terrified of her because I was too little to fight back. After she abused and humiliated me throughout the evening, she would try to be nice to me. Once everyone was asleep, she would wake me in the middle of the night to molest me. She made me think that when she touched me, it was her way of apologizing. She would ask me if I was mad. Once I refused to allow her to touch me and made it clear that I was angry, the physical abuse got worse.

When I see things on the news about kids dying from being kicked in the abdomen so hard that they had internal bleeding, I remember being kicked for the first time till the wind was knocked out of me. I weighed no more than 45 pounds. I felt defeated. I would give in to her sexual abuse thinking that maybe she would stop bullying me. She was about 16 years of age and very immature. She introduced me to fear and shame. She is the reason I didn't like myself. She brought sadness and stole my childhood joy.

I eventually grew up. I became a mother with two children by the age of 19, a son, and a daughter. I went through emotional and physical abuse from their father. Every few months, he cheated with a new chick assuming I was just going to stick around. Then one day he left us, and I was left to care for my babies alone. It was okay though because, by that time, I stopped loving him and myself anyway. I even attempted suicide to numb the pain. He reminded me of how dumb and stupid I was and instead of trying to help fix me, he threatened to take my kids away because I was unstable. Well, that helped me to get over him quickly and to realize that my children needed me to get it together. I had to be a mom regardless of whether he was going to treat me correctly. So, he left, and I moved on.

I got married at 25. I had two more children with my husband. During that hell of a marriage, I was abused, my children were abused, and it just seemed as though the situation couldn't get any worse. I could not understand why I was attracting people who didn't know or want to know how to love me lovingly. I finally realized that I just needed to get my children to a safe and loving home and living with him could possibly cost me my life. I prayed and asked God to get us out of that bondage. He rescued us from the lion's den, and we were safe.

Fast forward, nearly 18 years later, I am listening to the voice of God as He is guiding me as to what He wants me to say to you. He wants you to know how to love *you* correctly, as He is teaching me how to love me.

It is a hurtful thing to look in the mirror and not be able to genuinely love who you see. Then God reminds you that He lives on the inside of you and that you are looking into His eyes through the eyes He gave you. God can never be wrong. If He tells you that He loves you unconditionally and that you are beautiful, and that you are fearfully and wonderfully made, then you must learn to believe it for yourself. When He created life as mentioned in the book of Genesis, He wanted every living thing He created to be happy and free. He wanted us to love and be loved. He speaks of it several times throughout the Bible. We were created to always worship and honor Him as He pours down blessings upon us.

The enemy somehow convinced man to challenge God and to disobey Him. During our disobedience, we did things to dishonor ourselves, we hurt our loved ones, we hurt our neighbors, and we allowed the enemy to use us. The Ten Commandments gave us mandates to follow, in order for our lives to be full. Exodus 20:5-6 reads, "You shall not bow down to them or worship them; for I, the Lord your God, am a jealous God, punishing the children for the sin of the parents to the third and fourth generation of those who hate me, but showing love to a thousand generations of those who love me and keep my commandments."

Verses 12-21 list every detail about how God commands us to live in His Will. One of those Commandments requires us to love our neighbor as we love ourselves. The problem is, if we do not know how to properly love ourselves, it is impossible to love our neighbors correctly. There is a generational stigma being handed down through generations of families that causes some to have the spirit of self-hate and self-sabotage. This causes individuals to hurt others. It also causes us to allow others in our space, who abuse and mistreat us as well. We are soul-tied to individuals who were sent to tear us down and they don't love anyone, not even themselves. There are some deep-rooted, troublesome feelings created by our ancestral experiences. It is like the domino effect.

We were taught that everything bad that has happened to us, we experienced during slavery. This is the reason that it is so difficult to undo. There are several layers of hurt, hatred, misery, and unforgiveness buried in our culture and our spirit. As we grow and mature, we must learn how to expose and undo it all.

In studying, "What is Love?" I had to start with myself and my relationship with God. He loves us so much that He sacrificed His only begotten son so that we may be free and saved from sin. He gave us the instructions listed in the 10 Commandments. He gave us the Fruits of the Spirit, and He gave us His unconditional love. He grants us daily grace, mercy, and favor.

Some believe that love only relates to our feelings between man and woman. Some believe that love is sexual. True love involves so much more than that. If we learn the Fruits of the Spirit as we obey the Ten commandments, we will master the truth about love.

Love involves kindness, respect, support, and truthfulness. It requires honesty, patience, and forgiveness. Here is a list of the Twelve Fruits of the Holy Spirit: "

o   Charity is the voluntary giving of help.

o   Joy is a feeling of great pleasure and happiness.

o   Peace is a state of mental calmness and serenity,

o   Patience is the ability to accept or tolerate delay, trouble, or suffering without getting angry or upset

o   Kindness is selfless, compassionate, and merciful.

o   Goodness is an act of selflessness.

o   Generosity is a willingness to serve one another in love through giving our time, talents, or treasures.

o   Gentleness is the power of one's spirit that exudes meekness or mildness.

o   Faithfulness is the steadfastness, consistency, and commitment or allegiance

o   Modesty is the behavior, and manner, in which we avoid the appearance of impropriety or being indecent.

o   Self-control is the ability to control oneself within the Word of God according to following the Commandments

o   Chastity is refraining from extramarital sexual activities.

Although it seems as though we have fallen short of most of the things listed, we must do our best to follow these keys in order for our lives to be what God has intended for us. If we all knew the fruits of the Spirit and used them as our guidelines to steer us back into the love God wants us to experience, we will truly know What Love Is.

If we could just give ourselves a real chance at love, this world would be a much better place. Some don't believe it is possible to experience true love because they really don't know what that looks like. Hopefully, I will be able to shed some light on this topic. I am praying for myself and for you that we truly can understand love better than we ever have. I am praying that I can begin to truly feel the love of God on the inside of me. It will be evident when I see what God sees when I look at myself in the mirror. It will be evident when I see what God sees when I look at people. I will know it when I am able to look at my abusers, those who dislike me or hate me, the way God looks at them. Even though we error, He loves us all unconditionally. He will meet us where we are located and mold us into who we are proposed to be. His love covers all. He chastens whom He loves.

We must receive the Spirit of Obedience down on the inside of us. Our obedience is proof to God that we love Him also. Our obedience is our love offering to God. Following His commandments shows that we Trust Him and we Honor Him. Speaking is not enough. It is our actions that prove. Like the old cliché', *actions speak louder than words*. Although words have power, our actions activate the words we speak. He gives us the choice and the will to do. However, it is a requirement. I will commit daily to working on loving God, Me, and You correctly.

Write a list of daily affirmations to speak over yourself. Think of nice things you would like to believe about you. Allow your Spirit Man to work on the inside of you. Speak to yourself in the third person. Practice looking at yourself in the mirror. Say what makes you feel good. And then, practice saying it to others. Pay a compliment to another person passing by. A simple smile or hello will boost another person's self-esteem. It will also create an atmosphere that will invite joy and peace into the room.

Have you ever walked into a room and just blurted out good morning everybody? The look on everyone's faces would be a surprise because that is something they aren't used to. Most people are consumed with texting or scrolling down their timelines on social media. Some are engaged in deep thoughts, sometimes negative ones. Some are even thinking of giving up. Your smile and excitement of just saying good morning may change the entire room. You, alone, can put a smile on everyone else's heart. Love is infectious. Once you exhibit love, you will most definitely feel the love. The love of God will surround you and the people around you. And because of it...the enemy will have to leave the room.

The Power of... What Is Love??

Chapter Nine:

Exhale

Risa Jenkins

Risa Jenkins

"To start understanding my trauma I had to find a purpose to live. Reasons to want better. Make promises to try then vowing to fight for my life or die trying. It took me being a SURVIVOR to truly start putting things into perspective. More importantly, I had to learn that it was not my fault. It was not until I began to heal that I knew it was my duty to be a help to others. To be an ally, a resource...an advocate."

Rhianna's Treasured Gifts is a 501 (c) non-profit organization whose mission is to uplift and support victims of Domestic Violence.

RTG is committed to serving battered individuals to be an aide in the process towards healing, so they know that they have support and are not alone. All services are completely charitable in nature and are designed to help victims heal.

Rhianna's Treasured Gifts was established March 9, 2020.

They host consecutive donation drives monthly.

RTG made their 1st partnership with CAWC (Connections for Abused Women) by August 24, 2020

By November in 2020, RTG developed a mentorship program called "Breakthrough"

- A 12-week curriculum-based program that focuses on the youth who are left behind due to their demographics, adversaries or are economically impacted. Youth explore a variety of topics ranging from: Identity, Stress relief, Healthy coping, and Financial literacy

BY 2021 We were partnered with YCCS-West, ASN (Alternative School Network), Elite Treatment Center, Direct Distributors for Lisa Jenkins the creator of The SlipOut App, Christ Temple Baptist Church, Zakat Foundation of America, and Global Soku Foundation

She is a Mentor, Author, Advocate, Community Outreach Specialist, CEO and Founder of Rhianna's Treasured Gifts.

Exhale

Love- although an emotion, is a word used to express the depths and lengths you'll go for someone to prove your worth and even theirs. At least that's what I've come to learn.

There are several aspects of love. Let's dive deep as I briefly touch on ALL aspects of love. I was first introduced to love through my family and their "tough love" led me to searching for love romantically. That road led me to self-love and when I tell you I've never loved harder in my life, I stand on that!

My parents are from the south and moved up north with all their southern swag. Because times were so different growing up in the 60's they experienced everything about life from a completely different perspective. Old teachings and ways then carried over through parenting. What that looked like was being taught how to make a home, raise a family, and go to school. All things needed to mold you into being a perfect mate. Well, a perfect Christian wife that is. There wasn't much time for nurturing moments. You fall? Get back up! You failed? Try again! You're sad? Wipe your tears! You need a hug? Stop being so emotional! Depressed? Stop looking for attention! You're angry? That's the devil! Yeah- we flourished in tough love daily! We, as in my sister and I, were very close and are still thick as thieves.

Now when you're growing up in a Christian household, there is no conversations about intimacy. Just the constant reminder of abstinence, not committing adultery, no fornication, and no shacking. There were a LOT of no's with little to no explanation. We were sheltered and attended private school with the same people we went to church with. In fifth grade I transferred to a public school, and everything was so different. I was now exposed to "the world" as the church would say and I picked up on new habits very quickly. As a teenager attending a public school while living in a new neighborhood because you just moved to the suburbs is tripped out! I just left all my friends in the city, my sister (really my best friend) just left for college, my parents are older and I had to start this new 4year journey alone. During this time my parents and I didn't see eye to eye most days. Many would call this the rebellious stages, but I'll refer to it as my challenging ones. The power struggle was the wedge between my mother and I who at that time was the more active parent. My father, a military man was the type to have multiple jobs at once. He'd go in to work early and leave late but when he wasn't working, he was sleeping. As I met new people and began to make friends, naturally we compared households and upbringings. Our viewpoints on life were so different. My last year in high school I fell head over heels for someone. I just KNEW this was LOVE!! Ultimately, I end up moving out my parents' home at age 16 chasing after him. That relationship lasted two years and turned out to be my first abusive relationship. I gave him my all. I gave my checks, my car, my body, and my mind in efforts to prove my love. Nothing I did or sacrificed was ever enough. Ultimately, I escaped that life and ran to the Navy. I didn't know at the time I already had developed PTSD resulting in my separation a few months later. Fast forward three years, I was in a new entanglement and now pregnant. I lived a fast and reckless life up to this point, so I wasn't ready. Back when I was in that two-year relationship, I mentioned, the doctors told me I wouldn't be able to have children. February 14th, 2011 I took a test that would change my life forever. It was a positive pregnancy test and I couldn't believe it! My relationship was on the fritz and like most I thought it would save us. The moment I decided to go through with the pregnancy even after abandonment was the day I knew THIS was LOVE. I never so badly wanted to live for someone else. To care for someone other than my self because it was my job to do so. I wanted to be the best at it. This was a gift and despite not feeling worthy I was so humble and appreciative. September 9th, 2011, Rhianna was born prematurely. Weighing 3lbs I was told my baby wouldn't make it. My heart felt as if it shattered in a million pieces. I promised God I would change if he saved my baby's life. I did exactly that and she grew tremendously. A miracle, that's what they called her.

Regardless of what challenges I had ahead of me it didn't matter. My mind, heart and soul were set on winning no matter the cost. I gave my baby everything I had in me to give and soon I found out there's sometimes a cost to happiness. I wanted to give my child a family, so I got married not too long after she started walking. My then husband was not her father but he cared for her as if she was his own. They were inseparable and my little family was complete.

Although I was married, it was an experience I wouldn't wish for anyone. Who knew I was married to a addict who was also a habitual liar? Time after time and day after day we fought and argued when we weren't making up. It was one of those relationships that everyone envies because they only see what's happening on the outside and from other's perspective we were "goals". We were attractive, had money and enjoyed life. On March 18th I woke up to the day that changed it all. It was a day I'll never forget. After already having marital issues, I woke up that day to the news of the death of my brother. I found out on Facebook at that. Later that day I had to tell my family then my father. My husband worked overnights at the time, and I remember begging him to call off because I needed him. When he left for work, I was definitely livid, but I had no idea he wasn't coming back home and that I'd lose the child we conceived a couple months before. I didn't hear from him until a week later. Five minutes after putting my brother's body in the ground, he called drunk, asking for a divorce and once again my heart shattered into a million tiny pieces. The entire separation process was completely chaotic to say the least. Before the divorce was final, we lived separate lives and I had fallen for someone else but I didn't know it would be short lived. We both were existing outside of our unhappy marriages and the broken version of ourselves relied heavily on each other. Toxic wasn't the word to thoroughly describe our situation but soon deadly would be more appropriate.

That was the last time someone put hands on me. The last time I would allow harm to come close to my child. The last time I let anyone attempt to take my life! My wakeup call redefined my purpose and so I decided to LOVE ME for the first time.

How could I be deserving of love? If I'm not good enough for anyone else, how can I be good enough for me? WHAT THE HELL IS LOVE?? To find my answer I resorted to my roots and what I was taught as a child. Corinthians 13:4-8 *Love is patient, love is kind. It does not envy, it does not boast, it is not proud. It does not dishonor others, it is not self-seeking, it is not easily angered, it keeps no record of wrongs. Love does not delight in evil but rejoices with the truth. It always protects, always trusts, always hopes, always perseveres. Love never fails.*

For the first time, this passage made so much sense! I knew I had to make all necessary provisions ASAP. It started with counseling; it wasn't really my thing, but it was mandatory due to the program I was participating in. I got back on my feet after pulling myself out of what seemed to be the blackest, deepest hole on earth. Then I moved to a new neighborhood, started a new career and things start to get better. As years went by my daughter started to demand more out of life. She wanted to start an organization that helped other survivors of domestic violence. Little did she know I was completely terrified and ashamed of my truth. On top of that I didn't hold a degree higher than my high school diploma. So starting a business with ZERO experience mortified me. Seeing my baby's passion was like watching fire burn in her eyes so I knew what I had to do. I enrolled in school, obtained my degree then launched our organization, Rhianna's Treasured Gifts. To my surprise I still wasn't ready even after our approval.

I never healed from any of my traumas. I had so many unresolved issues and my mindset was still in survival mode. I realized I am no good to anyone if I am not okay. I knew I was still broken and that I held on to resentment.

From as far as I can remember I come from a place of anger, sadness, fear, hurt, and guilt. It was a lot of forgiveness of self I had to consider as well and that was HARD. So, now when you ask me what love is, what it looks like, feel like, or when I knew what it was, I can confidently say this..." I wouldn't be where I am today if it weren't for therapy." To get here, I first made an appointment with my therapist. This is where my "Love research" initiated. December 5th I was invited to an open house at Doorway 11. Who knew that day was when I'd meet my spirit guide in human form? My next mission was to find a way to get my therapist to see my thoughts and hear the words I was unable to articulate. Without hesitation and no idea on where to start or let alone approach her...I set my first appointment. It was a very painful yet brutally honest relationship I've ever encountered. Growing pains is truly a thing! A year later I was able to reflect on how much love I poured into myself by making my mental health a priority. I'm now able to move, think, and breath as "love".

Replace the word "love" with "I"

I am patient, I am kind. I do not envy, I do not boast, I am not proud. I do not dishonor others, I am not self-seeking, I'm not easily angered, I keep no record of wrongs. I do not delight in evil but rejoice with the truth. I always protect, always trust, always hope, always persevere. I never fail.

I was in a dark place, praying for strength to end it all, constantly begging for relief.

I now know my inner Divine is what saved me, what healed me.

As of late, I fell in love with tasks to maintain this healthy relationship I have with myself. I go on trios, I meditate, I do yoga, and I love on people unconditionally. I know I will continue to grow and excel. Throughout my life I have proven my ability in social perceptiveness and fostering positive relationships while promoting cultural competence. As I continue to actively look for ways to help people rather internal or external, I'm confident in my readiness. I take pride in being able to empathize, respect and be accountable while building a rapport with people over a multitude of situations. I'm intrigued by life and thrilled to LIVE. I know my life's experiences will aide in the healing of others.

So, Exhale...know that I love you. Beyond your flaws and deeper than your pain, I got you.

"Falling in love with yourself is the first secret to happiness"

-Risa J

The Power of... What Is Love??

Chapter Ten:

The Different Levels of Love

Latonya Willett

 **_Latonya Brown Willett_**, a Chicago native, born on the Westside of Chicago, is known to the reading and writing world as an 8-time author. She co-authored books that offers life lessons and motivation to women all over the world. Two of the 8 books co-authored are entitled, Because I Am More Than Just My Skin and The Birth to My Purpose.

In the the financial world, Latonya is known as The Money Lady. Her experience as a Financial Analyst has shaped and served her well with entrepreneurship. The Money Lady analyzes and presents budget plans, investment ideas, as well as provide insurance options.

Her 20 years of expertise in the financial industry and her previous background in nursing and sciences has been life-changing for her clients; so much so that she has won awards for her efforts and successes. Being recognized as one of the "100 Black Queen's of Chicago" is not only a result of her hard work and dedication, but she is humbled with the opportunity to be a part of such an elite group of professional women!

Mrs. Willett did not just arrive at such an epitome of service through happenstance. Next to the youngest of 4 children, even with several siblings, she still wanted to give to others. As young as 4 years old, Latonya always had a caring heart for others. Because she wanted others to feel as much love and care as possible, she chose what worked; giving of her time, money she was given for birthdays and holidays, toys, and anything else she was able to offer.

As Latonya grew more mature, she continued a caring spirit, but had to conquer life along the way. By the age of 14, she had her first child and by the time she was 17 she had her second child. While struggling to keep up her grades and take care of 2 children with the support of only her older sister, her second child would eventually die at the age of 4 months old on Mother's Day from SIDS. Only by the grace of God did
Latonya navigate her way through depression, suicide attempts, and still have a heart for those in need.

Four months after the death of her son, she met the man that would later become her husband. They have 2 sons together and 2 grandsons, one from the oldest and 1 from the middle son.

Latonya is the Outreach Director of her church as well as an ordained Evangelist, has her own Non-Profit called Blessings From Heaven. She also helps her 22-year-old son run both of his businesses: Dance Characters and BopKing

Larry Entertainment. The 2 of them travel to schools teaching the children about how money works and how they can become a business owner themselves.

Latonya, the real *Comeback Queen,* has grown to obtain a wealth of knowledge about life's hardships, overcoming obstacles, business, wealth creation, and legacy building.

Contact:

Latonya Willett | LatonyaWillett@yahoo.com

The Different Levels of Love

Love can be many different things to different people. Especially depending upon how they've experienced love. Let me explain. There's "Philia Love" – Affectionate Love, which is known as friendship or family love, often referred to as "brotherly love". There's "Pragma Love" – Enduring Love, the love that grows over time without even consciously knowing or trying. There's "Storage Love" – Family Love, the love between the parents and children, it happens immediately. There's "Eros Love" – Romantic Love; this is the love that needs the physical touch. There's "Ludus Love" – Playful Love, the love you feel when you're dating, beginning to date, or you want to inform someone that you're interested in them (flirting). There's "Mania Love" – Obsessive Love; this love is exactly as it states. This type of love often leads to toxic relationships where there's a possibility that someone can get seriously hurt. There's "Philautic Love" – Self Love; this type of love deals with knowing and acknowledging your self-worth and nurturing yourself in a healthy way. We also have "Agape Love" – Selfless Love; this is the highest level of love. This is a love that is unconditional and asks for nothing in return. It's often referred to as "Charity", because this is the love Jesus showed to everyone. This love can be demonstrated for a particular person or for humankind as a whole.

There are some people who have experienced love in its greatest and purest of forms, while there are others who have experienced love in the most toxic and perverted of forms. Today, I want to explore the ways in which I've experienced "Love".

One love I've experienced is the Storage and Agape love mixed. I experienced this love from my sister. When my child died from SIDS, the only person that was there for me during my time of sadness and self-destruction was my sister. We had just gone through this same kind of pain some years earlier when my brother lost his 1-year-old daughter to a house fire. Now, we were back here again with my 4-month-old son, DeAndre. How does one get over the death of a child, especially when they are yet a child themselves? How does one get over the fact that they want to leave this earth to be with their child when they still have another child that needs them? Well, you never really get over anyone dying, especially your child. You just gain better coping skills, whether it's through therapy, counseling, religion, a support system, or all of the above. I went to therapy which really helped me a lot. As for a support system, my sister was there for me to talk to. She was there for me when I needed to express my feelings. She was there to help with the child I still had to take care of while going to school and work. She was there to say, "You can do it. You can keep on going", when no one else was there to say those words or to show me that love I so desperately needed. During this time, I met my now husband. He was a good distraction from what I was going through at the time. I had someone that I could flirt with as well as someone who knew what I was going through and allowed me to express myself to him. Even after we were married, there were years where every January 4th, DeAndre's birthday, and Mother's Day, his death date. I would stay in the bed crying the entire day, but he was right by my side consoling me the entire time.

I have also had this kind of love for my son's as well as other family members and strangers. For the fact that I was in so much pain at such an early age, I always wanted to ensure no one else goes through pain, or at least not as much pain if there is something I can do to help. It's something about being a parent though. When you're a parent, you don't want to see your child in any pain at all, even though you know that pain is all a part of life and their growth in the learning process. You don't want them to fall off the bike, you don't want them to feel disappointment of any kind, whether it be from so called friends or significant others. As a parent you want to shield them from all the bad things that can happen in their life. Sometimes you can run them away because you're so intent on wanting what's best for them. I've found the best thing to do, is allow them to feel the pain of whatever life has to offer but be there when they need a shoulder to lean and cry on. Trials and tribulation will only make them stronger. You can be there for guidance if they ask for it, but you must trust the process.

I have shown love for many people that both could or could not do for themselves. Sometimes a person may need someone to step up for them when there is no one else there to do it, or even when they are in so much pain that they won't or cannot even do it for themselves. Sometimes life can deal you such a bad hand that you just don't want to be here anymore, let along care about how someone treats you. You may not even treat yourself in the way you should. I've found that when you're at your lowest point in life and just don't know which way to turn, God will always show His love and have a ram in the bush.

Throughout my years, I've also seen love that was not so good. The kind of love we call toxic love. The love where if person A doesn't do what person B wants in the relationship there's criticism, mockery, and downright mean displays, and actions of abuse. This not only happens between couples, but also between friends and family. This is so not healthy. This is the type of "love" that bleeds on everyone. It bleeds on the family members and friends who try to mediate the situation. Often, they are put in a position where they have to choose between the two parties involved. If there's any children involved or around to watch the turn of events it bleeds on the children especially, and in the worst way possible. These displays of abuse can lead a child to one of two things. The child will either want to be and do the exact opposite of what they're seeing and hearing, or it will show the child that this is how they should be treated or how they should treat others. This is where the generational problems/curses have an open door to come right in. It is so important to nurture your children and show them good healthy relationships with friends, family members, significant others, coworkers and with themselves as well. They need to see how they should take up for themselves when someone is trying to misuse them or belittle them. The sad part is a lot of people would never allow someone to treat another person unkind but would allow it for themselves repeatedly. This is something that must be stopped.

When a person knows their self-worth, there will be no one on the face of this earth that can tell them otherwise or make them feel any self-doubt, low self-esteem, or even take a second guess about themselves of any kind. That is the truest of self-care and self-love. When you love yourself, you can then truly love others. You can do this because you have taken time to stop and smell the roses. You have taken the time to slow down and listen to your heartbeat, your breathing, your body, your mind, and your spirit. You've taken the time to get to know yourself, find out what it is you like, the things you want out of life, the things that make you happy or even sad. All the things that make you who you are.

If you don't take care of yourself, how can you truly take good care of or love someone else? Think about it. If someone relies on you to give them love and to nurture them, but you don't love yourself enough to stop others from mistreating you, or if you don't love yourself enough to simply get proper rest when its needed, you will not be the best version of yourself to represent or advocate for that person. You'll be distracted from how you were treated earlier, or you'll be distracted by the sleepiness and fatigue you feel from not getting enough rest and something will go lacking.

You should also never downplay your talents and accomplishments to make someone else feel better about themselves. They should be your cheerleader. Whether it be a friend, significant other, coworker, or family member. When someone doesn't feel good about themselves unless you're feeling bad about yourself, that is a red flag that you are indulging in a toxic relationship.

The title of this book is, "What is Love?" From my point of view, love should be gentle, kind, understanding, compromising, always using healthy forms of communication. Love is accountability, flowing in integrity. Love should show grace when needed. Love is honest. Love should be pure and given freely, flowing straight from the heart. Love is the greatest gift that can be given. Love is free of charge, not wanting anything in return. Love is amicable. Love is healing to the soul. Love can heal a broken heart, and a grieving heart. Love has no boundaries. Love is capable of anything. Love can be used to take a person to their highest of heights. Love is respectful. Love is to be aware of one's needs or shortcomings and not use it against them. Love is having a compassionate heart for your fellow human being. Love is being able to have such a strong connection with someone that in their time of trouble, you can look at them and they know you have their best interest at heart. Love is being able to feel the presence of God. Love is security. Love can make you feel warm and fuzzy on the inside. Love is unconditional, it will catch you when you fall. Love is a learned behavior. Love is self-care. Love is awareness of oneself. Love is knowing what you want out of life and what you don't want out of life. Love is knowing what you'll accept and what you won't accept for yourself. Love can break down walls of confusion. Love is a force. Love is power. Love can give you the courage to become who you were always meant to be in life. Love nurtures, it's like marrow to your bones.

Now, for what love is not. Love does not bring shame. Love does not boast or brag. Love should never be overbearing or isolating. Love does not belittle or put down. Love does not leave you guessing about your place in a person's life. Love should not be forced. Love is never anger. Love is not impatient. Love is never abusive, whether it be verbal, mental, physical, or emotional. Love does not keep you in bondage. Love is not cruel. Love does not play with your heart. Love is not competition.

I've given the different levels and types of love. It is up to you to know if the type of love you're receiving is healthy for you or not. If you find that the love being given, or the love you are giving is not of the purest form, you need to do something about that. Maybe seek counseling at your local church. Seek therapy from a therapist, but if it's worse than that, do not hesitate to call the National Domestic Violence Hotline at 800-799-7233. You are not alone. There are people who can help. Once you know better, you must do better.

Chapter Eleven:

Loving Me Some Me

Luberta Lytle

Luberta Lytle is a Christian Certified Life Coach and the owner/proprietor of L.L. Life Coaching Company. She is also the founder and executive director of Dorothy Johnson My Biggest Fan, NFP. In addition to her career as a life coach, she recently retired from working with the Illinois State Government after 32 years. She is currently serving on the Board of Directors for the SAFE and CASA of Marion County Organization. She is also serving as an Ambassador for the Centralia Chamber of Commerce.

Before anything else, Ms. Lytle is a mother of three, grandmother of eleven, and just recently became a great-grandmother. Luberta lives in Centralia, IL.

She is an avid reader and enjoys taking walks in her spare time and her heart is fueled by a passion for inspiring and motivating women.

 Luberta has proven her qualifications as a life coach as she has reached several successes over the past 30+ years of her career and life with her family. She has an MBA from Lindenwood University, a B.S. in Organizational Leadership from Greenville College, and a Practical Nursing Certification from Kaskaskia College.

Luberta is an author and co-author of several books. Just in case you hadn't read, she just recently obtained another Amazon Best-Selling book title, plus an Amazon Best-Selling International book for her chapter in As For Me and My House. She became a 1st-time author after her first solo project called, Heal the Hurt.

During her writing career, Luberta penned a chapter in the Jabez Readers' Choice Award-winning book, Millionaire M.O.M.: Living Dreams, Transforming Lives, and Defying the Odds of Teen Motherhood and co-wrote The She-Preneur Journey, and penned a chapter in the Amazon Best-Selling book #BossMoms.

Deservingly so, Ms. Lytle has recently accepted the role of Vice-President for AFSCME 31 Retiree Sub-Chapter. She received the BPW of Marion County Distinguished Women of the Year award and is currently traveling with and featured as one of the speakers with the Art of Transparency, NFP organization. She lovingly shares her stories of overcoming, the various obstacles throughout her life. Her contribution to helping women change the trajectory of their life's plans and goals has had enough impact to where everyone she encourages has made the first steps for change: *obtaining a positive mindset.*

www.lubertalytle.com |
https://www.facebook.com/CoachBerta/ | 618-237-4130

luberta@lubertalytlelifecoach.com

Loving Me Some Me

I remember seeing the title, What's Love for the first time. I thought what do I think about love? Love has not been a part of my life since 1988. My mother passed away on May 25th of 1988 at 5:27 pm. After the passing of my mother, I stop accepting or receiving love. My mother was the only person, that absolutely loved me. I was upset with God, because he took away the one person, really loved and cared for me. He left me motherless at the age of twenty-one and this pain was just too, hard to bear. Nobody prepares you for living without your parent. Nobody tells you that you will always, miss this person. Nobody tells you that a part of you die when your mother dies. I was alone in this world with three small children to raise. I was not prepared mentally or physically to raise these kids, because I could not get over losing my own mother. I became cold and could not care less about what happened around me. I was just existing, not living.

This hurt and sadness, lead me to make some desperate decision, which lead to a lot of disappointment. I had three children and two baby daddies. I should have just stayed single and raise my children on my own, but they needed some stability. After, thinking things over, me and one of my baby daddies, decided that we should get married. I knew in my heart that this was not a good decision, but I thought that this would help ease some of my pain and hurt. I realized the day of the wedding, that this one a mistake. Three years after losing my mother, I got married.

I still had not come to grips or terms with this loss. I just pushed into the back of my mind and thought that this distraction would make it go away. I was so wrong, with this thought process. My mother had been gone for three years and I decided to get married on her birthday.

My mother's birthday is on Valentine's Day. The most romantic day of the year. I really wish that I can say that I got married for love, but that would be a lie. I got married to ignore my pain and hurt, hoping that it would give my children some stability. This marriage was a mistake and the only good thing that out of it was, our two children. I could put allow of the blame on him, but it truly takes two people to make or break a marriage. We both had our own hidden agenda for getting married, but neither one of us did it for love. We both had our hurt and pain, that we had not or would not deal with in our own lives. We both were two hurt adults, hurting each other. Our marriage lasted approximately three years, but the life lessons from that marriage lasted for several years. I had not come to terms with the loss of my mother's death and added this failed marriage into my baggage. I had genuinely believed at this time, that love did not exist in my life. This marriage and relationship caused more heart ache than it brought joy. I believed everything negative thing that was shared with me during this relationship. I believed that nobody would want me for anything, other that sex. I believed that I would never be enough for any man. I believed that no other man would every find me desirable. I believed everything negative thing that this man told me. I finally decided to leave after three years, but the mental damage had already been done. Me not thinking that I was good enough, lead me to desperate decision and disappointment number two. I should have taken this opportunity to heal from the hurt from my life, but instead I moved right into another relationship. It was just another distraction, which would give me another life lesson. This relationship was with an older man. We started out as friends and should have keep our friendship. I thought that because he was older and more established, we would be okay. I never thought about the fact, that we both needed to heal from the hurt and pain from our lives. We were just some more broken adults, hurting other broken adults. I thought that because he was not physically abuse that this relationship would be different. I thought that because he held a decent paying job, that this relationship would be different. I thought that we would just be could for each other. You noticed that I have not said, anything about love. I did not think about love regarding this relationship, this one centered around security for me. I believed that we could live our separate lives and come together when we needed too. We lived like this for most of our relationship and it worked for us. We did not put any pressure on each other, we just did our own thing. We decided that since we had been involved for ten years, it was time to get married. Our marriage was not based on love, it was centered around us believing that we needed to stop living in sin. This was the second marriage for both of us. Nobody had taken the time to heal from the first marriage. Nobody had taken the time heal from our past hurt. Nobody had taken the time to decide what we wanted out of a relationship or marriage. We instead brought all our baggage and mess into this marriage. We never became married in life, just on paper. We never became united, we remained separate. We never made each other a priority. We never made the sacrifice to fight for our marriage. We only stayed married because nobody wanted to look like a failure. We held onto the marriage, because of our pride and ego, not for love. This marriage went on for fifteen years. We had been friends for over thirty years. Everything that I shared with me as my friend, he used against me in our marriage. Every insecurity that I had about myself, he threw it up in every argument. The issues that caused me hurt and pain in my first marriage, he did in my second marriage. I believed everything that he told me. I was hard to love. My personality was too strong. I was unapproachable. He was my last hope for happiness. I believed without him I would be alone. He was the only person who cared for me. I believed that if we would break up, I would be all alone. I believed everything that he told me, because I felt and saw myself in the same way. I had allowed myself to believe that this was the best that I could do. I still believed that love did not exist for me. He was my knight and shining arm, that if I gave him enough time he would change and love me some me. Our marriage was already over, before we said, I do.

I made the decision that enough was enough. I decided that it was time for me to love me. I started changing and growing. I made the decision after fifteen years of marriage and thirty years of being in a loveless relationship, that it was time for something different.

I have shared the bad side of what love is not, but I have learned what love is. I have learned that I will always miss my mother, but she would prefer that I love myself, instead of being sad. I have learned that I am not alone but loved by God. He loves me despite my shortcomings. Yes, he was ready for my mother to come back home, but she completed her assignment before she left. She gave and showed me the correct way to give and receive love. I just decided to create and live inside my own mental pity party. I decided to make the wrong decision and choices regarding my relationships. I decided to believe the negative things that my ex-husbands told me. I decided to stay in those marriages and relationships. It was easier to accept and believe what they said, because I did not want to deal with my own foolishness. I finally had to look in the mirror and apologize to myself for believing all the lies. I had to tell myself that it was time for healing and moving on. I had to tell myself that it was time to Let Go and Let God. I finally decided that it was time for me to love me. I have tried so many other things, but never wanted to love me. I am finally doing something for me. If I do not love me, I cannot expect anyone else to do it. I have decided that it is time to release myself from myself and start over again. I have decided that all the love my mom gave me, I will start back using it for me. I have decided that it is time for me to remove the negative words instilled in my memory bank and start replacing them with positive words. I heard a song a song, called I Love Me Better Than That, by Shirley Murdock. This song talks about a woman who has endured physical and mental abuse from past relationships. It talks about how her life has caused her to question her own sanity. She finally decides, that enough is enough, and she is going to take control back over her life. She builds up all her strength and starts moving forward. I listened to the words of this song and realized that this song was talking about my life. I realized in that moment that I Had Control Over MY LIFE.I realized it would take ME to Determine How I Received Love. I Decided in the moment, that No one who keep me prisoner. I decided in that moment that I would start Loving Me. I decided in that moment that I deserved to be Loved. I decided in that moment that my Life mattered. I decided that I would stop giving power to all the negative things shared me about throughout my adult life, but instead start feeding myself with positive things. I decided that my life did matter, and I deserved everything good that could come from it. I decided in that moment that I was not alone, and nobody loved me, but instead that my heavenly father loved me unconditionally. What is Love for me? The excitement that I get when I wake up in the morning knowing that God loves me and that I am loving me some me. Knowing that I am loved by God and myself means the world to me, because for so long I believed that I could not or deserved to be loved by anyone. So, if anyone else decides to love me than, they will consider a bonus person. If it happens cool, but I know realize that it is more important for me to love me than waiting and/or expecting it to come from someone else. I will continue to keep on loving me some me

If we elect not to love ourselves with all our faults and insecurities, then why would we put that expectation on someone else?

Take the time to heal from past hurt. Free yourself from yourself. Know yourself worth and add tax on it. Be open and honest with yourself, regarding what type of relationship you are desiring. Do not make desperate relationship and/or life decision, because they will truly lead you down a path of disappointment.
Remember you are IN CONTROL OF HOW YOU RECEIVE AND GIVE LOVE!!!!

The Power of... What Is Love??

Conclusion

Thank you for taking the time to purchase and read "The Power of... What Is Love??"

In this anthology, we the Authors, wanted to share our story of what love means, looks like, feels like from the perspective of a woman. This love is not just romantic, but it's about motherly love, friendship love, the just all-around love. We want you to know that you are not alone in this journey. This love thing has so many twists and turns, so many ways to heal, deal and learn while learning what it is. Please KNOW that love looks, feels, and is reciprocated in all kinds of ways. Your love may very well look much different than anyone else.

For the **BIBLE** says:

- John 3:16: For God so loved the world, that he gave his only Son, that whoever believes in him should not perish but have eternal life.

- Romans 12:9: Love must be sincere. Hate what is evil; cling to what is good.

- Colossians 3:14: And over all these virtues put on love, which binds them all together in perfect unity.

- Jude 1:2: Mercy, peace and love be yours in abundance.

And these are just a few scriptures about *Love*. We have to remember that God is a keeper of all things and will never forsake us. Your right now is for somebody else's tomorrow. We stand to help others behind us.

Remember that your prayers are being heard. You have to continue to heal and grow into yourself, continue to have faith in knowing that God is working on your behalf. It will all work out in due time, in due season, and all in God's timing…. Continue to do the *WORK*.. Therapy, long hard conversations, taking the look in the mirror… If you continue to do the work, God will most amazingly do the rest.

Thank you!

Invisible Daughter LLC

Under the umbrella of Mikkita Moore LLC

www.mikkitamoore.com

Notes...

The Power of... What Is Love??

The Power of... What Is Love??

Made in the USA
Middletown, DE
15 May 2022

65796352R00086